Christian Moral Life

A Primary Source Reader

Ann Nunes

saint mary's press

The publishing team included Gloria Shahin, editorial director; Jeanette Fast Redmond, development editor. Prepress and manufacturing coordinated by the production departments of Saint Mary's Press.

Cover Image @ The Crosiers / Gene Plaisted, OSC

Printed in the United States of America

1363

ISBN 978-1-59982-140-5, print
ISBN 978-1-59982-472-7, Kno
ISBN 978-1-59982-260-0, Saint Mary's Press Online Learning Environment

Contents

"Canticle of the Creatures," by Saint Francis of Assisi

"Anima Christi" and *"Suscipe,"* from the *Spiritual Exercises,* by Saint Ignatius of Loyola

Introduction

Therefore, since we are surrounded by so great a cloud
of witnesses, let us rid ourselves of every burden and sin
that clings to us and persevere in running the race that
lies before us while keeping our eyes fixed on Jesus, the
leader and perfecter of faith. (Hebrews 12:1–2)

Imagine that you are running a race in a crowded stadium. Feel the
pounding of your feet against the track. Just a quarter of the way
into the race, you start to feel tired and wonder if you can even
make it to the finish line.

Suddenly you begin to hear your name called from the stands.
People are cheering you on, but you do not know who they are.
They are calling your name, saying: "You can make it! It's in you!
Keep going! You can win!" Who *are* these people? How do they
even know your name? Why are they so confident that you can
even finish the race, much less win?

It is working, though. You can feel their confidence in you, as
if the wind is at your back. You can make it. You might even win!

In the moral race too—the race to overcome sin and be a
faithful follower of Christ—there is a crowd cheering us on. The
Letter to the Hebrews calls this cheering crowd a "cloud of witnesses" (12:1). They are the voices of the holy men and women
throughout history who have gone before us marked with the sign
of faith. They have persevered. They have run the good race. They
have claimed their prize and are now cheering us on as we run
life's race. They are calling us to victory.

This cloud of witnesses is part of a larger community that the
Church calls the Communion of Saints. We are one family that
looks out for one another: asking for help from those who can give
it, and giving help to those who need it. Heaven and earth are
united in this familial reality, the Communion of Saints.

All the members of this family have your back as you run life's
moral race. You do not have to run it alone. The Christian moral

life is defined by loving relationships. Human relationships are not always the image of perfect love, and we sometimes feel discouraged and disappointed by people in our lives. We may feel weary with our relationships and think we have no one to turn to. But we have God. God is always there and wants us to know that we have many more friends than social networks could ever count—for we are part of the Communion of Saints. We are supported by faithful people—living and dead—who can offer us insight about running life's moral race.

This primary source reader, *Christian Moral Life*, includes letters, sermons, and other writings of many holy people. Each of the reader's four parts begins with a reading from a contemporary moral theologian. These modern authors are then followed by others in the cloud of witnesses, that great crowd of faithful men and women who are cheering you on.

- Part 1 considers what we mean when we talk about "life in Christ." In these readings Blessed John Paul II, Julian of Norwich, the Blessed Virgin Mary, and others examine the fulfillment of God's promises in Christ and what it means to respond with love, just as Mary said yes to God's plan.
- Part 2 goes on to discuss how God taught us to live this new life in Christ. The Two Great Commandments and the Beatitudes are among the topics explored here by Blessed John Henry Newman, Blessed Teresa of Calcutta, Saint Thérèse of Lisieux, Pedro Arrupe, SJ, and others.
- Part 3 examines how this new life in Christ and the Gospel message are at the heart of Catholic moral teaching. Selections from Hildegard of Bingen, Saint Thomas More, Saint Alphonsus de Liguori, and others talk about the virtues, the importance of developing and following one's conscience, and the role of prayer in making moral decisions.
- Finally, Part 4 explores the reality of sin through the writings of self-professed sinners like Saint Augustine and Saint Teresa of Ávila. But their readings, as well as sermons from Saint John

Vianney and Archbishop Oscar Romero, also call us to conversion and cheer us on with the hope of redemption.

Two thousand years of Church history are represented through these writings. Although each author reflects the period of time in which he or she wrote, every author shares wisdom that transcends time and place, wisdom that is relevant to your moral life today.

Although many authors in this book have departed this life, they are very much alive and present to you in spirit. If you open your ears and your heart, you will know they are cheering you on. They really do have your back. They can help you run life's moral race with your eyes fixed on Christ.

Part 1

Created in the Image of God, Who Is Love

1 Loving the Good Life

Introduction

"The good life"—what images come to mind when you think of that phrase? The reading in this chapter comes from a book called *The Good Life: Where Morality and Spirituality Converge*, by Fr. Richard Gula, a moral theologian, professor, and author known for considering modern questions and dilemmas through the eyes of faith in Jesus Christ. While writing *The Good Life*, Gula took an informal survey that posed a similar question about this phrase. As you read the selection in this chapter, see how your idea of "the good life" lines up with that of others.

This introductory reading begins with the idea that love makes the good life possible. According to Gula, despite what popular culture may tell us, the good life is one of communion with God, who is always extending his divine hand in love and friendship. Jesus Christ is God's love in the flesh; Christ shows us how to be good friends with God the Father. Throughout the Gospel of John, Jesus calls his disciples "friends" and instructs them, "As I have loved you, love one another" (John 13:34). The good life is therefore a life of giving and receiving love.

Although abundance does mark the good life, constantly changing media images and values surround us with only an illusion of abundance. Gula reminds us that the steadfast and abundant love of God is already within us. If we are open to it, this love becomes a wellspring to help us live authentically as people of character and virtue. When we live authentically in the image of God, in whom we are created, and when we embody the love of God in the world today, we walk the moral path. Rooted in this reality of divine love, our moral actions flow from the essence of who we are—or rather, whose we are. God invites us to be his friends. If we accept this invitation, our morality is defined by this friendship. Morality is relational; that is, our relationships with

right relationships Relationships aligned to help each human being to thrive in mind, body, and spirit.

vocation A call from God to all members of the Church to embrace a life of holiness.

God, with others, and with ourselves inform our moral choices.

As a professor of ethics and moral theology, Gula has taught that this relational understanding of morality is central. Any student who has walked into his introductory class on moral theology anticipating a dry recitation of regulations and rules in the Catholic Church has been pleasantly surprised to discover that he really teaches guidelines about being in **right relationships** that are rooted in the love of God as revealed in the life of Jesus Christ. Through his **vocation** as a priest, as well as his speeches, classroom teaching, and many published books, Gula has guided people of all ages to recognize God's love at work in their lives and to respond with character, virtue, and moral integrity—in essence, to lead good lives.

Morality, the truly good life, is rooted in love. Christian morality is synonymous with life in Christ. As Gula explains in the following excerpt, "The good life for a Christian takes its shape from our allegiance to Jesus the Christ" (p. 6). This allegiance forms and transforms our character so that we truly love living the good life.

Excerpt from *The Good Life: Where Morality and Spirituality Converge*
By Richard M. Gula, SS

"Someone in Nebraska loves me." So read the bumper sticker on the car in front of me while I was driving along one of California's freeways this afternoon. I thought, what a great way to begin this short book on the moral life. After all, being loved makes the moral life possible! For the moral life is really about living out of the abundance of being loved in ways that make life richer for everyone. How are we ever going to live in ways that promote the well being and full flourishing of ourselves and others, as well as the whole environment, if we do not first feel the love of another for us?

Now, Nebraska is a long way from California, but that distance quickly shrinks with the thought that someone there holds us close to their heart. To know that someone loves us, that we are special to them, not only brings them close to us but also strengthens, consoles, and empowers us to live out of the gifts that are ours. It is so much easier to take the risk to love another, even a stranger, when we know that someone, somewhere, loves and cherishes us.

As the experience of lovers tells us, loving another and being loved by another creates a dynamism that opens us beyond the particularity of the one we love and moves us outward toward the goodness and lovableness of all people—in fact, of all creation. The moral life depends on the experience of being loved and on the dynamic pull that draws us to love all things, and ultimately to love God.

. . . Spiritual masters throughout the ages have told us in a variety of ways that God's love for us does not compete with the relationships we have with other people or creation. We do not have to step over or around them in order to get to God. Rather, God comes to us in and through our relationships with all things.

But to say "God loves you!" may seem trite. We have heard it so many times that it may very well suggest an empty piety. Yet, the good news of the Christian faith is that God's love is real, creative, constant, and undefeatable. God's loving us is the supreme truth, the rock bottom foundation, the **first principle** on which we build a moral and spiritual life. As with any first principle, we cannot prove it but we can deduce from it. Once we accept it, we can see how much follows from it. We can see that all of life is lived in the presence of God, is a response to God, and has value in relation to God's love.

first principle A foundational principle from which other truths can proceed.

The good life, then, is a graced life—a life that expresses the divine love within us. But is that what you really think of when you hear the expression "the good life"? . . . I took an informal survey of spontaneous associations of the good life. Images that most frequently surfaced were all influenced by the commercialism of our popular culture—owning a luxury car or a mountain villa, taking an exotic vacation or a cruise, being treated with first class service, dining in gourmet restaurants, and drinking fine wine.

These images came as no surprise because television and commercial ads are usurping the role of religion and the church in shaping our imaginations and our system of values. The kind of life they promote is often based on anti-Christian values such as greed, consumerism, and elitism. These contradict Christian teaching about **solidarity**, about standing with the poor, and about being a beatitude people. Christians, however, believe that the images that come to us in our religious stories provide truthful ways of seeing the world and ordering our values and that to use religious stories and images for interpreting what is going on can help us to engage the world as a people formed by Christian faith.

The good life . . . is fundamentally a vocation—a response to what we hear God speak to us. What we hear and how we respond are influenced by Christian stories and images. The good life is possible because God has made the first move. Our moving toward God begins with God moving outward into creation toward us, preeminently in Jesus but also in and through all the people and events of our lives. From the perspective of vocation, wherein God calls and we respond, the basic question governing the good life is "What is God calling us to be and to do?" The relationship we establish with God in and through our responses to all things becomes the center of the good life. The mystery of grace assures us that divine love is always with us, inviting us and leading us toward the realization of the fullness of life in communion with God. Living the good life, simply put, is graced living expressing the divine love within us.

solidarity Union of one's heart and mind with all people; a principle of Catholic social teaching based on the well-being of all people and the concept of the common good.

Christian spirituality and Christian morality converge in the good life. Spirituality is concerned with the wellspring of our actions. If we focus only on the actions that get done, then we neglect what nourishes and sustains those actions. There is more to us, and more to life, than what we do. Our interior life affects our exterior behavior. If we understand that the purpose of life is to live in friendship with God, then there can be no real separation of the moral and spiritual life. Our searching for meaning, hungering for love, yearning to connect, or seeking fulfillment are, themselves, responses to God's self-giving love.

For many people, however, the moral and spiritual life remain in two separate spheres. Some locate the spiritual life in the world of devotions, such as taking time for prayer or fasting. A spiritual life of this sort can easily become a substitute for vital moral living. But spirituality is much more about our fundamental commitment to God in Christ; it is an outlook on life and the very style of life that such a commitment nurtures in us.

When we separate morality and spirituality into separate spheres of life, we begin to reduce the moral life to sins or individual acts of virtue in specific areas of life—business dealings, sexual relations, making life-and-death decisions, and the like. We expect morality to provide a set of rules or principles that we only need to apply in order to determine the right way to act. In fact, so many books about morality still put the spotlight on individual acts, rules, principles, problems, and strategies for resolving them and then leave the nobler life to spirituality. But so much of our everyday moral living does not fall within those realms marked off by clearly defined rules or principles for direct action.

. . . Just as one's spirituality cannot be reduced to one's discipline of prayer, so the moral life cannot be reduced to acts or summed up in the decisions we make and the justifications we give to support the way we solve our problems.

Our ability to identify a problem, and even more to solve it, is a measure of who we are and how we live in the meantime. . . .

> " *When it comes to living the good life, character and virtue matter.* "

[My teaching concerns] the kind of persons we ought to become and the kind of life we ought to live from day to day by virtue of our commitment to God in Christ and through the Spirit. In this sense, the moral life has to do with what also pertains to spirituality—a deeper vision of life, basic attitudes toward life, and the style of life that is grounded in our commitment to God. . . . When it comes to living the good life, character and virtue matter; that is to say, the moral life and spiritual life converge when we begin to explore the sort of persons we ought to become and the sort of lives we ought to live in order to flourish as authentic human beings.

While emphasizing character and virtue, I am not advocating that the normative **morality of duty** and principles be dismissed. Virtue, duty, and principles are complementary aspects of the same morality. Virtues express those habits, affections, attitudes, and convictions that lead to genuine human fulfillment, that is, to being one with God and so with one another and with the environment. With virtue, we carry out religious devotions or do our moral duty not because someone is commanding us to do them or is keeping a watchful eye over us to assure that we do them. Rather, with virtue, we act out of an internal, self-directing commitment to the values at stake. Virtue ethics stresses that who we are overflows into what we do. Virtues link us to action by providing a sensitivity to what is right and a motivation to do what human well-being demands. Whether or not an obligation is prescribed by duties or principles, and whether or not anyone is watching, virtue makes us alert and responsive to the

morality of duty Actions based upon moral obligations rather than virtue or love.

moral claims of situations, often with little attention to rationalizing, calculating, or counting the cost. With virtue, we act naturally. We do not ponder, argue, or fuss. We simply move.

What is making a perspective from character and virtue so necessary? For one thing, our world is changing very rapidly. There is no way we could ever have answers today to questions and issues that we will have to face in the future. We don't even know what those questions and issues are going to be. Think back only thirty years or so. Who would ever have thought that we would now be facing what to do with frozen embryos, whether we ought to clone humans, or how to protect privacy or prevent harassment over the Internet? But by directing our attention to virtuous character, we may become the sort of people who will be able to make right decisions on matters that we have never anticipated. To this end, we will have to illuminate the background issues of the moral life, such as our moral vision, attitudes, motivations, affections, intentions, convictions, and habits that give a particular shape to our lives. When we highlight these aspects of our selves, we are illuminating our spirituality as well.

. . . [My] conviction is that the good life is a life of friendship with God and that we will become friends with God and with one another to the extent that we develop our character and virtues. . . . The good life for a Christian does not derive from some general concept of the good, such as what is pleasurable or useful. Rather, the good life for a Christian takes its shape from our allegiance to Jesus the Christ, whom we believe to be the decisive revelation of God's love for us and the fullest human response to that love. By freely entering into relationship with Jesus through the power of the Holy Spirit, we become disciples today. As such, we share in the life of love offered by God the Father. Every love changes us, but only God's love for us changes us into God's friends. This friendship with God will only be completely realized in heaven, that is, when the reign of divine love comes in its fullness.

Among the deepest questions we face in the meantime are questions about the meaning of life, about the sort of person we ought to become, and about how we ought to conduct our lives. In and through the biblical witness, especially the preaching, teaching, and works of Jesus, we see what life looks like when pointed in the direction of being a friend of God and of one another.

For Reflection

1. According to Gula, what is the "supreme truth," the "first principle," on which a Christian moral and spiritual life is built? Why might this be considered a first principle?

2. Compare and contrast the moral and spiritual life, as explained in this excerpt.

3. Based on what Gula says in this reading, what is replacing religion in shaping our values? What kind of life do these replacements promote, and how do they compare to Christian teachings? Do you agree or disagree with the author?

4. From the perspective of vocation, what does Gula say is the basic question governing the good life? How would you answer that question?

2 The Divine Embrace

Introduction

"We love you, John Paul Two! We love you!" chanted a crowd of Catholic university students during Pope John Paul II's first visit to the United States. Spontaneously he responded, "John Paul Two, he loves *you*!" The 263rd successor to Saint Peter has been called the "Pope of the Youth." The world's youth were near to his heart; he frequently called young people his dear friends.

Named Karol Wojtyła at his birth in 1920, Blessed John Paul II was destined to live a **cosmopolitan** life in every sense. The most traveled Pope in history, he visited 130 countries during his pontificate and spoke at least seven languages fluently. At his invitation 160 religious leaders of various faith traditions worldwide came to Assisi, Italy, for the first World Day of Prayer for Peace. And he initiated World Youth Day, inviting young people from around the world to gather in host cities (such as Denver, Paris, Manila, Sydney, and Madrid) for a joyful celebration of faith and culture.

This chapter's excerpt comes from Pope John Paul II's message to young people at the fifteenth World Youth Day, held in 2000 in Rome. The scriptural theme running through all the events of that World Youth Day was adapted from the Gospel of

World Youth Day

In 1986 young people from around the world accepted Pope John Paul II's invitation to come celebrate their faith with him in Rome. World Youth Day was born. Each year since, young people of faith have gathered for WYD either in their dioceses for a day or on weeklong pilgrimages in host cities around the world. The world's youth who embark on the WYD journey joyfully share the diversity of their cultures and the unity of their faith.

John: "The Word became flesh, and dwelt among us" (1:14). The theme was a reminder that God's promise and plan are to dwell among us, lovingly embrace us, and share with us the happiness of Heaven.

In this reading Pope John Paul II encourages us to open our hearts to God's plan of love, revealed most fully in the life, death, and Resurrection of Jesus. He seeks to inspire us to be faithful to the Christian message, to live in solidarity, and to be cosmopolitan in the Christian sense—united with people of every culture through God's redemptive love. He reminds us that the cross of Christ—the symbol of Christian **redemption**—brings together Heaven and earth. The outstretched arms of Jesus on the cross envelop all of humanity and tenderly hold the cosmos "in a divine embrace" (2). The Passion of Christ demonstrates this divine love and reminds us that God intimately knows our human suffering. Through our own sorrows and suffering, we too can know Jesus Christ.

Pope John Paul II calls us to be **saints**: "May it be your holy ambition to be holy, as He is holy" (3). As God is holy, we are called to be holy, to be *sancti*, to be saints. Just as Christ sent forth the Apostles to proclaim his Good News two thousand years ago, the Pope sends us forth to build a new humanity founded on the love and forgiveness received in the divine embrace of Christ.

cosmopolitan Having a worldly outlook or broad cultural frame of reference.

redemption From the Latin *redemptio*, meaning "a buying back," referring, in the Old Testament, to Yahweh's deliverance of Israel and, in the New Testament, to Christ's deliverance of all people from the forces of sin.

saints From the Latin *sanctus*, meaning holy; someone who has been transformed by the grace of Christ and who resides in full union with God in Heaven. In this reading, it refers to being saintly or holy people here and now.

Excerpt from "Message to the Youth of the World on the Occasion of the Fifteenth World Youth Day"

By Blessed John Paul II

2. . . . I make again to you my pressing appeal to open wide the doors to Christ who "to those who received him, gave power to become children of God" (*Jn* 1:12). To receive Jesus Christ means to accept from the Father the command to live, loving Him and our brothers and sisters, showing solidarity to everyone, without distinction; it means believing that in the history of humanity even though it is marked by evil and suffering, the final word belongs to life and to love, because God came to dwell among us, so we may dwell in Him.

By his incarnation Christ became poor to enrich us with his poverty, and he gave us redemption, which is the fruit above all of the blood he shed on the Cross (cfr *Catechism of the Catholic Church* 517). On **Calvary**, "ours were the sufferings he bore . . . he was pierced through for our faults" (*Is* 53:4–5). The supreme sacrifice of his life, freely given for our salvation, is the proof of God's infinite love for us. Saint John the Apostle writes: "God loved the world so much that he gave his only Son so that everyone that believes in him may not be lost but may have eternal life" (*Jn* 3:16). He sent Him to share in every way, except sin, our human condition; he "gave" him totally to men, despite their obstinate and homicidal rejection (cfr *Mt* 21:33–39), to obtain, through his death, their reconciliation. "The God of creation is revealed as the God of redemption, as the God who is 'faithful to himself' and faithful to his love for man and the world which he revealed on the day of creation . . . how precious must man be in the eyes of the Creator, if he gained so great a Redeemer" (*Redemptor hominis* 9.10).

Jesus went towards his death. He did not draw back from any of the consequences of his being "with us," *Emmanuel*. He took our place, ransoming us on the Cross from evil

Calvary The place outside the city walls of Jerusalem where Jesus was crucified.

and sin (cfr *Evangelium vitae* 50). Just as the Roman Centurion, seeing the manner in which Jesus died, understood that he was the Son of God (cfr *Mk* 15:39) so we too, seeing and contemplating the Crucified Lord, understand who God really is, as he reveals in Jesus the depth of his love for mankind (cfr *Redemptor hominis* 9). "Passion" means a passionate love, unconditioned self-giving: Christ's passion is the summit of an entire life "given" to his brothers and sisters to reveal the heart of the Father. The Cross, which seems to rise up from the earth, in actual fact reaches down from heaven, enfolding the universe in a divine embrace. The Cross reveals itself to be "the centre, meaning and goal of all history and of every human life" (*Evangelium vitae* 50).

"One man has died for all" (2 *Cor* 5:14): Christ "gave himself up in our place as a fragrant offering and a sacrifice to God" (*Eph* 5:2). Behind the death of Jesus there is a plan of love, which the faith of the Church calls the "mystery of the redemption": the whole of humanity is redeemed, that is, set free from the slavery of sin and led into the kingdom of God. Christ is Lord of heaven and earth. Whoever listens to his word and believes in the Father, who sent him, has eternal life (cfr *Jn* 5:25). He is the "Lamb of God who takes away the sins of the world" (*Jn* 1:29.36), the high priest who, having suffered like us, is able to share our infirmity (cfr *Heb* 4:14) and "made perfect" through the painful experience of the Cross, becomes "for all who obey him, the source of eternal salvation" (*Heb* 5:9).

3. Dear young people, faced with these great mysteries, learn to lift your hearts in an attitude of contemplation. Stop and look with wonder at the infant Mary brought into the world, wrapped in swaddling clothes and laid in a manger: the infant is God himself who has come among us. Look at Jesus of Nazareth, received by some and scorned by others, despised and rejected: He is the Saviour of all. Adore Christ, our Redeemer, who ransoms us and frees us from sin and death: He is the living God, the source of Life.

Contemplate and reflect! God created us to share in his very own life; he calls us to be his children, living members of the mystical Body of Christ, luminous temple of the Spirit of Love. He calls us to be his: he wants us all to be saints. Dear young people, may it be your holy ambition to be holy, as He is holy.

You will ask me: but is it possible today to be saints? If we had to rely only on human strength, the undertaking would be truly impossible. You are well aware, in fact, of your successes and your failures; you are aware of the heavy burdens weighing on man, the many dangers which threaten him and the consequences caused by his sins. At times we may be gripped by discouragement and even come to think that it is impossible to change anything either in the world or in ourselves.

Although the journey is difficult, we can do everything in the One who is our Redeemer. Turn then to no one, except Jesus. Do not look elsewhere for that which only He can give you, because "of all the names in the world given to men this is the only one by which we can be saved" (*Acts* 4:12). With Christ, saintliness—the divine plan for every baptized person—becomes possible. Rely on Him; believe in the invincible power of the Gospel and place faith as the foundation of your hope. Jesus walks with you, he renews your heart and strengthens you with the vigour of his Spirit.

Young people of every continent, do not be afraid to be the saints of the new millennium! Be contemplative, love prayer; be coherent with your faith and generous in the service of your brothers and sisters, be active members of the Church and builders of peace. To succeed in this demanding project of life, continue to listen to His Word, draw strength from the Sacraments, especially the Eucharist and Penance. The Lord wants you to be intrepid apostles of his Gospel and builders of a new humanity. In fact, how could you say you believe in God made man without taking a firm position against all that destroys the human person and the family? If you believe that Christ has revealed the

Pope John Paul II and the Saints

During his twenty-six-year pontificate, Blessed John Paul II canonized more saints than any other Pope in modern history. He wanted the people of our time and of all nations to have models of faith and spiritual friends for life's journey. During his own lifetime, John Paul II touched the hearts of so many that when he died in 2005, people around the world spontaneously cried out, *"Santo Subito!"* ("Sainthood now!") He was beatified in 2011, the first step toward possible canonization.

Father's love for every person, you cannot fail to strive to contribute to the building of a new world, founded on the power of love and forgiveness, on the struggle against injustice and all physical, moral and spiritual distress, on the orientation of politics, economy, culture and technology to the service of man and his integral development.

4. . . . From the whole Church may there rise up "a hymn of praise and thanksgiving to the Father, who in his incomparable love granted us in Christ to be 'fellow citizens with the saints and members of the household of God'" (*Incarnationis Mysterium* 6). May we draw comfort from the

> 66 *With Christ, saintliness—the divine plan for every baptized person—becomes possible.* 99

certainty expressed by Saint Paul the Apostle: If God did not spare his only Son but gave him for us, how can he fail to give us everything with him? Who can separate us from the love of Christ? In every event of life, including death, we can be more than winners, by virtue of the One who loved us to the Cross (cfr *Rom* 8:31–37).

The mystery of the Incarnation of the Son of God and that of the Redemption he worked for all men, constitute the central message of our faith. The Church proclaims this down through the centuries, walking "amidst the misunderstandings and persecutions of the world and the consolations of God" (*S. Augustine De Civ. Dei* 18, 51, 2; PL 41,614) and she entrusts it to her children as a precious treasure to be safeguarded and shared.

You too, dear young people, are the receivers and the trustees of this heritage: "This is our faith. This is the faith of the Church. And we are proud to profess it, in Jesus Christ Our Lord" (Roman Pontifical, *Rite of Confirmation*).

For Reflection

1. According to the Pope, what proves the infinite love God has for us? In your own words, explain why this is considered proof of God's love. How does he say we should respond to this proof?

2. John Paul II calls all of us to be "the saints of the new millennium." What are we called to do? How can you personally respond to this summons?

3. Based on this reading, what is the central message of our faith?

3 Our Divine Dignity

Introduction

What does a boomerang do when it is thrown? It returns to its starting point. Saint Athanasius could be considered a human boomerang. Five times he was exiled for his unrelenting defense of the Council of Nicaea's teaching that Jesus Christ was both true God and true man. This was a perilous effort in fourth-century Alexandria, Egypt, where he was bishop, but he would not give in to the **heretical** religious pressures of his day. The Nicene Creed, the great Christian proclamation of faith that came out of the Councils of Nicaea and Constantinople, affirms the teaching of Nicaea and Athanasius's defense of it. Through this creed we avow that the Son is both true God and true man, and we profess belief in one God who is Father, Son, and Holy Spirit.

At the heart of the mystery of the **Trinity** is the truth that the Father (the Creator), the Son (the Redeemer), and the Holy Spirit (the **Sanctifier**) are in perfect communion with one another and that their work and mission are inseparable. Each acts to create us in love, redeem us, and make us holy. However, "each divine person performs

heretical Related to a conscious and deliberate rejection of a dogma of the Church.

Trinity From the Latin *trinus*, meaning "threefold," referring to the central mystery of the Christian faith that God exists as a communion of three distinct and interrelated divine Persons: Father, Son, and Holy Spirit. The doctrine of the Trinity is a mystery that is inaccessible to human reason alone and is known through Divine Revelation only.

Sanctifier One who makes something or someone holy; another title for the Third Person of the Trinity.

the common work according to his unique personal property" (*Catechism of the Catholic Church*, 258).

The three readings in this chapter are from three of the Greek Church Fathers of the third and fourth centuries: Saints Athanasius (297–373), Gregory of Nazianzen (329–374), and Basil the Great (329–379). Gregory and Basil, lifelong friends and intellectual giants in the Eastern Church, followed in the footsteps of Athanasius as champions of Church teaching on the Persons of the Blessed Trinity. Recall how the Book of Genesis reveals our creation in the image of God—in Latin, *imago Dei*. The **Incarnation** and the sending of the Holy Spirit reveal that God is a Trinity of Divine Persons. More accurately, then, we are created in the image of the Trinity, *imago Trinitatis*. Each of these readings from the Greek Fathers explores the unique properties of one of the Persons of the Trinity.

The first excerpt comes from *On the Incarnation of the Word*, Saint Athanasius's best-known **apologetic** writing. In this selection he defends teachings on the eternal existence of the Word of God; and he explains how, in the Incarnation, the Word became human for our redemption. Through Jesus Christ's life, death, and Resurrection, "the law of corruption" is destroyed, meaning that death and bodily decay do not have the final word. Rather than signifying the end of life, death has become the beginning of life eternal because Christ on the cross restored the immortality and glory of humanity, as seen in his Resurrection. In short, Jesus Christ became man so that we might share in his divinity.

Incarnation From the Latin, meaning "to become flesh," referring to the mystery of Jesus Christ, the divine Son of God, becoming man. In the Incarnation, Jesus Christ became truly man while remaining truly God.

apologetic Refers to a literary form in which one defends a position, often religious in orientation.

The second reading in this chapter is from a sermon by Saint Gregory of Nazianzen, who calls us to appreciate the manifest generosity of God the Father, the First Person of the Trinity, to whom we owe our very existence. When he created us in his image, God granted us an abundance of beauty and the blessings of the earth as divine gifts to be enjoyed and shared with others. Gregory reminds us, as children of God and "coheir[s] with Christ," that we are called to be generous with these divine gifts and not to abuse them.

Saint Basil the Great is the author of the last reading in this chapter, from his treatise on the Holy Spirit. The Spirit, he reminds us, is the source of all holiness and is the light of truth that empowers us to grow in God's grace. By becoming more perfect windows into the divine presence within us, we become channels of the Holy Spirit. Like Athanasius, Basil speaks of our own divinity when he explains that we become God through the Spirit.

As you read these selections, consider the significance of your identity as a human being created in the image of God. Think about how your life is affected by the grace of the Resurrection, how you express generosity toward creation, and how you are a source of grace for others. Christian morality means living out our capacity to act in the image of God and to share in the life of the divine Trinity.

Excerpt from a Discourse, *On the Incarnation of the Word*

By Saint Athanasius

The Word of God, incorporeal, incorruptible and immaterial, entered our world. Yet it was not as if he had been remote from it up to that time. For there is no part of the world that was ever without his presence; together with his Father, he continually filled all things and places.

Out of his loving-kindness for us he came to us, and we see this in the way he revealed himself openly to us. Taking pity on mankind's weakness, and moved by our corruption, he could not stand aside and see death have the mastery over us; he did not want creation to perish and his Father's work in fashioning man to be in vain. He therefore took to himself a body, no different from our own, for he did not wish simply to be in a body or only to be seen.

If he had wanted simply to be seen, he could indeed have taken another, and nobler, body. Instead, he took our body in its reality.

Within the Virgin he built himself a temple, that is, a body; he made it his own instrument in which to dwell and to reveal himself. In this way he received from mankind a body like our own, and, since all were subject to the corruption of death, he delivered this body over to death for all, and with supreme love offered it to the Father. He did so to destroy the law of corruption passed against all men, since all died in him. The law, which had spent its force on the body of the Lord, could no longer have any power against his fellowmen. Moreover, this was the way in which the Word was to restore mankind to immortality, after it had fallen into corruption, and summon it back from death to life. He utterly destroyed the power death had against mankind—as fire consumes chaff—by means of the body he had taken and the grace of the resurrection.

This is the reason why the Word assumed a body that could die, so that this body, sharing in the Word who is above all, might satisfy death's requirement in place of all. Because of the Word dwelling in that body, it would remain incorruptible, and all would be freed for ever from corruption by the grace of the resurrection.

In death the Word made a spotless sacrifice and oblation of the body he had taken. By dying for others, he immediately banished death for all mankind.

In this way the Word of God, who is above all, dedicated and offered his temple, the instrument that was his body, for us all, as he said, and so paid by his own death the debt that was owed. The immortal Son of God, united with all men by likeness of nature, thus fulfilled all justice in restoring mankind to immortality by the promise of the resurrection.

The corruption of death no longer holds any power over mankind, thanks to the Word, who has come to dwell among them through his one body.

Excerpt from a Sermon, "Let Us Show Each Other God's Generosity"
By Saint Gregory of Nazianzen

Recognize to whom you owe the fact that you exist, that you breathe, that you understand, that you are wise, and above all that you know God and hope for the kingdom of heaven and the vision of glory, now darkly and as in a mirror but then with greater fullness and purity. You have been made a son of God, coheir with Christ. Where did you get all this, and from whom?

Let me turn to what is of less importance: the visible world around us. What benefactor has enabled you to look out upon the beauty of the sky, the sun in its course, the circle of the moon, the countless number of stars, with the harmony and order that are theirs, like the music of a harp? Who has blessed you with rain, with the art of husbandry, with different kinds of food, with the arts, with houses, with laws, with states, with a life of humanity and culture, with friendship and the easy familiarity of kinship?

Who has given you dominion over animals, those that are tame and those that provide you with food? Who has made you lord and master of everything on earth? In short, who has endowed you with all that makes man superior to all other living creatures?

Is it not God who asks you now in your turn to show yourself generous above all other creatures and for the sake of all other creatures? Because we have received from him so many wonderful gifts, will we not be ashamed to refuse him this one thing only, our generosity? Though he is God and Lord he is not afraid to be known as our Father. Shall we for our part repudiate those who are our kith and kin?

Brethren and friends, let us never allow ourselves to misuse what has been given us by God's gift. If we do, we shall hear Saint Peter say: *Be ashamed of yourselves for holding on to what belongs to someone else. Resolve to imitate God's justice, and no one will be poor.* Let us not labor to heap up and hoard riches while others remain in need. If we do, the prophet Amos will speak out against us with sharp and threatening words: Come now, you that say: *When will the new moon be over, so that we may start selling? When will sabbath be over, so that we may start opening our treasures?*

Let us put into practice the supreme and primary law of God. He sends down rain on just and sinful alike, and causes the sun to rise on all without distinction. To all earth's creatures he has given the broad earth, the springs, the rivers and the forests. He has given the air to the birds, and the waters to those who live in water. He has given abundantly to all the basic needs of life, not as a private possession, not restricted by law, not divided by boundaries, but as common to all, amply and in rich measure. His gifts are not deficient in any way, because he wanted to give equality of blessing to equality of worth, and to show the abundance of his generosity.

Excerpt from a Treatise, *On the Holy Spirit*
By Saint Basil the Great

The Work of the Holy Spirit

The titles given to the Holy Spirit must surely stir the soul of anyone who hears them, and make him realize that they speak of nothing less than the supreme Being. Is he not called the Spirit of God, the Spirit of truth who proceeds from the Father, the steadfast Spirit, the guiding Spirit? But his principal and most personal title is the Holy Spirit.

To the Spirit all creatures turn in their need for sanctification; all living things seek him according to their ability. His breath empowers each to achieve its own natural end.

The Spirit is the source of holiness, a spiritual light, and he offers his own light to every mind to help it in its search for truth. By nature the Spirit is beyond the reach of our mind, but we can know him by his goodness. The power of the Spirit fills the whole universe, but he gives himself only to those who are worthy, acting in each according to the measure of his faith.

Simple in himself, the Spirit is manifold in his mighty works. The whole of his being is present to each individual; the whole of his being is present everywhere. Though shared in by many, he remains unchanged; his self-giving is no loss to

> " *Through the Spirit we acquire a likeness to God; indeed, we attain what is beyond our most sublime aspirations— we become God.* "

himself. Like the sunshine, which permeates all the atmosphere, spreading over land and sea, and yet is enjoyed by each person as though it were for him alone, so the Spirit pours forth his grace in full measure, sufficient for all, and yet is present as though exclusively to everyone who can receive him. To all creatures that share in him he gives a delight limited only by their own nature, not by his ability to give.

The Spirit raises our hearts to heaven, guides the steps of the weak, and brings to perfection those who are making progress. He enlightens those who have been cleansed from every stain of sin and makes them spiritual by communion with himself.

As clear, transparent substances become very bright when sunlight falls on them and shine with a new radiance, so also souls in whom the Spirit dwells, and who are enlightened by the Spirit, become spiritual themselves and a source of grace for others.

From the Spirit comes foreknowledge of the future, understanding of the mysteries of faith, insight into the hidden meaning of Scripture, and other special gifts. Through the Spirit we become citizens of heaven, we are admitted to the company of the angels, we enter into eternal happiness, and abide in God. Through the Spirit we acquire a likeness to God; indeed, we attain what is beyond our most sublime aspirations—we become God.

For Reflection

1. Saint Athanasius reminds us that Christ "took to himself a body, no different from our own." According to Athanasius, why did Christ take a human body?

2. What are some of the gifts of God that Saint Gregory names? How are we called to respond to those gifts?

3. Saint Basil compares the Holy Spirit to the sun to describe how the Spirit works in every human person. In your own words, explain your understanding of the truth that Basil is communicating with this analogy.

4 Christ's Lovers

Introduction

"Here is a vision shown by the goodness of God to a devout woman, and her name is Julian, who is a recluse at Norwich and still alive, A.D. 1413, in which vision are very many words of comfort, greatly moving for all those who desire to be Christ's lovers" (chapter 1).

So begins *Showings*, Julian of Norwich's written account of visions that God granted her during a severe illness. Her sixteen visions, or "showings," were mystical revelations about the nature of God's divine love for humanity. From a literary standpoint, *Showings* is thought to be the first book written in English by a woman. Little is known about Julian's life, but historians believe that she was a Benedictine **contemplative** nun who took her name from Saint Julian Church in Norwich, England, where she lived.

> **Love and *Agape***
>
> Julian writes much about love—God's love for us, and our love for God and others. Julian was influenced by a biblical understanding of love. The word for love used most frequently by Jesus in the Gospel narratives, which were written in Greek, is *agape*, a word that means unconditional and selfless love of others.

Throughout her writings Julian of Norwich expresses a desire that we experience a God who created, loves, and protects each of us. With such an experience, our response must naturally be to love God in return. The perfect model of a loving response to God is our Lady, the Blessed

> **contemplative** Member of a religious order devoted to prayer, personal sacrifice, and solitude.

Virgin Mary, mother of Jesus. In the first vision described in these excerpts, Julian sees Mary and the "reverent contemplation with which she beheld her God" (chapter 4).

The role of contemplation in our human life is important to Julian. As you read, keep in mind that God is speaking to you through her. Although the life you live is very different from hers, and the distance of time and place is vast, do not dismiss her writings as irrelevant to your own experience. Rather, translate her experience for your life today. You may not be called to abandon the created things of this world out of love for God, as Julian was—but God certainly is asking you to recognize that complete contentment cannot come from created things. It is only in the "love of uncreated God," as Julian says here (chapter 4), that the deepest desires of the human heart are satisfied. Julian's writings are one pathway to an encounter with this love.

Julian says that God gave her these visions for "the comfort of us all" (chapter 6). All of us have had times when we have wanted someone to comfort us, to say, "Everything is going to be okay." *Showings* is a revelation of reassurance. Amid her personal suffering and the general hardships common to her time, God communicated divine care and comfort through the mystical visions she experienced. In an oft-quoted passage from *Showings* (not included in this excerpt), God proclaims to Julian, "But all will be well, and every kind of thing will be well" (chapter 13). Through the **mysticism** of Julian of Norwich, God speaks those reassuring words today to all of us who desire to be Christ's lovers.

mysticism An intense experience of the presence and power of God, resulting in a deeper sense of union with God; those who regularly experience such union are called mystics.

Excerpts from *Showings*

By Julian of Norwich

Chapter 1

Here is a vision shown by the goodness of God to a devout woman, and her name is Julian, who is a recluse at Norwich and still alive, A.D. 1413, in which vision are very many words of comfort, greatly moving for all those who desire to be Christ's lovers. . . .

Chapter 4

And at the same time as I saw this corporeal sight, our Lord showed me a spiritual sight of his familiar love. I saw that he is to us everything which is good and comforting for our help. He is our clothing, for he is that love which wraps and enfolds us, embraces us and guides us, surrounds us for his love, which is so tender that he may never desert us. And so in this sight I saw truly that he is everything which is good, as I understand.

And in this he showed me something small, no bigger than a hazelnut, lying in the palm of my hand, and I perceived that it was as round as any ball. I looked at it and thought: What can this be? And I was given this general answer: It is everything which is made. I was amazed that it could last, for I thought that it was so little that it could suddenly fall into nothing. And I was answered in my understanding: It lasts and always will, because God loves it; and thus everything has being through the love of God.

In this little thing I saw three properties. The first is that God made it, the second is that he loves it, the third is that God preserves it. But what is that to me? It is that God is the Creator and the lover and the protector. For until I am substantially united to him, I can never have love or rest or true happiness; until, that is, I am so attached to him that there can be no created thing between my

> *God is the creator and the lover and the protector. For until I am substantially united to him, I can never have love or rest or true happiness.*

God and me. And who will do this deed? Truly, he himself, by his mercy and his grace, for he has made me for this and has blessedly restored me.

In this God brought our Lady to my understanding. I saw her spiritually in her bodily likeness, a simple, humble maiden, young in years, of the stature which she had when she conceived. Also God showed me part of the wisdom and truth of her soul, and in this I understood the reverent contemplation with which she beheld her God, marvelling with great reverence that he was willing to be born of her who was a simple creature created by him. And this wisdom and truth, this knowledge of her creator's greatness and of her own created littleness, made her say meekly to the angel Gabriel: Behold me here, God's handmaiden. In this sight I saw truly that she is greater, more worthy and more fulfilled, than everything else which God has created, and which is inferior to her. Above her is no created thing, except the blessed humanity of Christ. This little thing which is created and is inferior to our Lady, St. Mary—God showed it to me as if it had been a hazelnut—seemed to me as if it could have perished because it is so little.

In this blessed revelation God showed me three nothings, of which nothings this is the first that was shown to me. Every man and woman who wishes to live contemplatively needs to know of this, so that it may be pleasing to them to despise as nothing everything created, so as to have the love of uncreated God. For this is the reason why those who deliberately occupy themselves with earthly business, constantly seeking worldly well-being, have not God's rest in their hearts and souls; for they love and seek their rest in this thing which is so little and in which there is no rest, and do not know God who is almighty, all wise and all good, for he is true rest. God wishes to be known, and it pleases him that we should rest in him; for all things which are beneath him are not sufficient for us. And this is the reason why no soul has rest until it has despised as nothing all which is created. When the soul has become nothing for love, so as to have him who is all that is good, then is it able to receive spiritual rest. . . .

Chapter 6

Everything that I say about myself I mean to apply to all my fellow Christians, for I am taught that this is what our Lord intends in this spiritual revelation. And therefore I pray you all for God's sake, and I counsel you for your own profit, that you disregard the wretched worm, the sinful creature to whom it was shown, and that mightily, wisely, lovingly and meekly you contemplate God, who out of his courteous love and his endless goodness was willing to show this vision generally, to the comfort of us all. And you who hear and see this vision and this teaching, which is from Jesus Christ for the edification of your souls, it is God's will and my wish that you accept it with as much joy and delight as if Jesus had shown it to you as he did to me. I am not good because of the revelation, but only if I love God better, and so can and so should every man do who sees it and hears it with good will and proper intention. And so it is my desire that it should be to every man the same profit that I asked for myself, and was moved to in the first moment when I saw it; for it is common and general, just as we are all one; and I am sure that I saw it for the profit of many others. For truly it was not revealed to me because God loves me better than the humblest soul who is in a state of grace. For I am sure that there are very many who never had revelations or visions, but only the common teaching of Holy Church, who love God better than I. If I pay special attention to myself, I am nothing at all; but in general I am in the unity of love with all my fellow Christians. For it is in this unity of love that the life consists of all men who will be saved. For God is everything that is good, and God has made everything that is made, and God loves everything that he has made, and if any man or woman withdraws his love from any of his fellow Christians, he does not love at all, because he has not love towards all. And so in such times he is in danger, because he is not at peace; and anyone who has general love for his fellow Christians has love towards everything which is. For in mankind which will be saved is comprehended all, that is, all that is made and the maker of all; for God is in man, and so in man is all. And he who thus generally loves all his fellow Christians loves all, and he who loves thus is safe. And thus will I love, and thus do I love, and thus I am safe—I write as the representative of my fellow Christians—and the more that I love in this way whilst I am here, the more I am like the joy that I shall have in heaven without end, that joy which is the God who out of his endless love willed to become our brother and suffer for us. And I am sure that anyone who sees it so will be taught the truth and be greatly comforted, if he have need of comfort. . . . What I am saying I have received by the revelation of him who is the sovereign teacher. But it is truly love which moves me to tell it to you, for I want God to be known and my fellow Christians to prosper, as I hope to prosper myself, by hating sin more and loving God more. . . .

Chapter 9

God showed me three degrees of bliss that every soul will have in heaven who has voluntarily served God in any degree here upon earth. The first is the honour of the thanks of our Lord God which he will receive when he is delivered from pain. This thanks is so exalted and so honourable that it will seem to him that this suffices him, if there were no other happiness. For it seemed to me that all the pain and labour which all living men might endure could not earn the thanks that one man will have who has voluntarily served God. As to the second degree, it is that all the blessed in heaven will see the honour of the thanks from our Lord God. This makes a soul's service known to all who are in heaven. And for the third degree, which is that the first joy with which the soul is then received will last forevermore, I saw that this was kindly and sweetly said and revealed to me: Every man's age will be known in heaven, and he will be rewarded for his voluntary service and for the time he has served, and especially the age of those who voluntarily and freely offer their youth to God is fittingly rewarded and wonderfully thanked.

And after this our Lord revealed to me a supreme spiritual delight in my soul. In this delight I was filled full of everlasting surety, and I was powerfully secured without any fear. This sensation was so welcome and so dear to me that I was at peace, at ease and at rest, so that there was nothing upon earth which could have afflicted me.

This lasted only for a time, and then I was changed, and left to myself, oppressed and weary of myself, **ruing** my life so that I scarcely had the patience to go on living. I felt that there was no ease or comfort for me except hope, faith and love, and truly I felt very little of this. And then presently God gave me again comfort and rest for my soul, delight and security so

ruing Regretting, feeling remorse for.

blessed and so powerful that there was no fear, no sorrow, no pain, physical or spiritual, that one could suffer which might have disturbed me. And then again I felt the pain, and then afterwards the joy and the delight, now the one and now the other, again and again, I suppose about twenty times. And in the time of joy I could have said with Paul: Nothing shall separate me from the love of Christ; and in the pain, I could have said with Peter: Lord, save me, I am perishing.

This vision was shown to me to teach me to understand that every man needs to experience this, to be comforted at one time, and at another to fail and to be left to himself. God wishes us to know that he keeps us safe all the time, in joy and in sorrow, and that he loves us as much in sorrow as in joy. And sometimes a man is left to himself for the profit of his soul, and neither the one nor the other is caused by sin. For in this time I committed no sin for which I ought to have been left to myself, nor did I deserve these sensations of joy; but God gives joy freely as it pleases him, and sometimes he allows us to be in sorrow, and both come from his love. For it is God's will that we do all in our power to preserve our consolation, for bliss lasts forevermore, and pain is passing and will be reduced to nothing. Therefore it is not God's will that when we feel pain we should pursue it, sorrowing and mourning for it, but that suddenly we should pass it over and preserve ourselves in endless delight, because God is almighty, our lover and preserver.

For Reflection

1. What three properties did Julian see in the small round object in her hand? What do those properties tell her about God? What do they say about us in relation to God?

2. One of Julian's visions was a series of feelings alternating between joy and suffering. What did she learn from that experience?

3. Which of the visions or teachings did you find most compelling? Explain why it interests you. What did you learn from it, and how can you apply it in your own life?

5 Blessed Are the Meek and the Pure of Heart

Introduction

Have you ever been told, "You can catch more flies with honey than with vinegar"? Most people have heard that expression in one form or another, but fewer people know the man to whom it is attributed: Saint Francis de Sales.

Francis de Sales (1567–1622) studied at the best universities of sixteenth-century Europe, and his family anticipated that he would have a stellar career in government. However, he came to reject his father's wishes and instead entered the priesthood during the Protestant Reformation, a time of conflict and division inside and outside the Church. He responded to adversaries with loving words and kind actions. His friends scolded him for not dealing more harshly with those who opposed the Church, but Francis responded that he would rather be held accountable to God for too much gentleness than for too much severity. He acknowledged that he struggled with a quick temper; but very few witnessed his internal conflict, because Francis truly practiced what he preached. Through his deliberately gentle and meek manner, Francis de Sales brought many into the Catholic faith.

In the reading in this chapter, from his *Introduction to the Devout Life,* Francis explains what it means to be meek and humble, and he advises us to try to avoid anger. He reminds us of the example of Jesus Christ, who in the Gospels describes himself as "meek and humble of heart" (Matthew 11:29).

beatific Holy or blessed. Here, used to describe a life that follows the values taught in the Beatitudes, the teachings of Jesus from the Sermon on the Mount that describe actions and attitudes that lead to genuine meaning and happiness.

42

Jesus was a master teacher, and Francis learned from his example. Just as Jesus used details from everyday life in first-century Palestine to illustrate profound truths to his followers, Francis uses the common experiences of European life in his day as metaphors to illustrate lessons in humility.

Through Francis's imagery, the Beatitudes are brought to life. Found in the Sermon on the Mount in the Gospel of Matthew (5:3–12), the Beatitudes are at the heart of Jesus' teaching. They are guidelines for living the Christian life, telling us how we can best love and serve God and neighbor. In this excerpt Francis teaches that mildness—or meekness, in the language of the Beatitudes— helps us to be more loving toward our neighbors. When anger arises, instead of counting to ten before talking (as today we are often advised to do), Francis counsels us to call out to God for help, as did King David. He offers other do's and don'ts on the **beatific** path of gentleness: Do not let the sun set on your anger. Do not allow anger to lodge in your heart, where it could stay and influence who you become. Speak words of gentleness so that you are filled with gentleness. A person living according to the Beatitudes does not merely act with meekness and purity of heart, but rather *is* meek, gentle, and pure of heart.

More than four centuries have passed since *Introduction to the Devout Life* first circulated among laypeople, for whom it was written. Although he wrote for people of another time and place, the "Gentle Doctor" of the Church can teach us much today about the role of meekness and humility in a moral life.

Excerpt from *Introduction to the Devout Life*

By Saint Francis De Sales

Meekness and the Remedies for Anger

The holy Chrism used in the Church by Apostolic tradition for Confirmation and blessings is composed of olive oil and balm; thus representing, amongst other things, two of the most precious and blessed virtues which were conspicuous in our Saviour, and which He has enjoined on us as the special means of serving and imitating Him. "Learn of Me," He said, "for I am meek and humble of heart." Humility perfects us towards God, mildness or gentleness towards our neighbor. The balm which (as I have before said) always falls to the bottom when mixed with other liquids, represents humility, and the olive oil, which always rises to the top, represents gentleness and mildness which rises above all else, and excels among virtues, being the flower of charity, which St. Bernard pronounces to be perfect when in addition to being patient it is gentle and amiable. But give good heed that this precious oil of mildness and humility be within your heart, for one of the great wiles of the enemy is to lead men to rest content with the external signs of these virtues, and, without searching their inward affections, to think that because their words and looks are gentle, therefore they themselves are humble and mild, whilst in truth they are far otherwise. This is evident when, in spite of their show of gentleness and humility, they start up in wounded pride at the slightest insult or vexatious word. It is said that those who take the medicine called **St. Paul's cure**, will not, if it be pure, suffer from swelling with the viper's bite; and so if our humility and gentleness are genuine, they will preserve us from the swelling and inflammation which insult is **wont** to provoke in our hearts. If, then, when we are bitten and stung by our enemies and slanderers, we become proud, swollen, and indignant, it is a sure sign that our humility and meekness are false and artificial, not hearty and genuine.

When the holy Patriarch Joseph dismissed his brethren on their homeward journey, he charged them, "Be not angry in the way" (*Gen.* 45:24). This present life is but the road to a blessed life, let us not be angry on the way one with another; let us go forward with our brethren and companions gently, peacefully, and lovingly. I exhort you earnestly never to give way to anger; and never, under any pretext whatever, let it effect an entrance into your heart. St. James says explic-

St. Paul's cure Refers to the biblical story in Acts 28:1–6 in which Saint Paul was bitten by a viper but suffered no harm.

wont Having a tendency or inclination to do something.

itly that "the anger of man worketh not the justice of God." Undoubtedly, we must oppose what is wrong, and steadfastly check the vices of those under our care, but we must do so quietly and gently. Nothing appeases the elephant when irritated so much as the sight of a lamb, and nothing breaks the force of a cannonade so well as wool. The correction which is administered through passion, although reasonable, will not be as effectual as if reason alone were the instigator; for the reasonable soul is naturally subject to reason, but tyranny only subjects it to passion; and wherever reason is accompanied by passion, it is rendered hateful in proportion, and its just empire is lowered by its unworthy society. The peaceful visit of a prince gratifies and comforts his people, but when he is accompanied by an army although it may be for the public good, these visits are very unacceptable and mischievous, since, however strictly military discipline is observed, it is impossible always to insure that none shall suffer unjustly. So, whilst reason reigns and administers its reproofs, corrections, and chastisements, albeit with strictness and severity, it is loved and approved; but if it is accompanied by anger, wrath, and passion . . . , it becomes more an object of terror than of love, and it will be resisted and disliked. It is better (says **St. Augustine**, writing to Profuturus) to exclude wholly even the slightest wrath, albeit just and reasonable, for once having entered the heart it is hard to dislodge; especially though it enters in but a **mote**, it speedily waxes great and becomes a very **beam**. For if it abides with us, and, contrary to the Apostle's injunction, the sun goes down upon our wrath, and it is turned into hatred, we can no longer set ourselves free, for then it will be fed by a thousand false fancies and delusions; inasmuch as no angry man ever thinks his anger unjust.

It is safer, then, to avoid all anger, rather than to try and guide our anger with discretion and moderation; and if through our frailty and weakness

St. Augustine Fourth-century bishop of Hippo, acclaimed spiritual writer, and Doctor of the Church.

mote, beam From the Sermon on the Mount described in Matthew 7:1–5, in which Jesus teaches us not to judge others: "Remove the wooden beam from your eye first; then you will see clearly to remove the splinter [mote] from your brother's eye" (v. 5).

we are sometimes overtaken, it is better to resist it decidedly, than to try and make terms; for if once we yield ever so little, our anger will gain the upper hand, and like the serpent, easily drag his body where once he has inserted his head. Do you ask how to resist anger? As soon as you feel the slightest resentment, gather together your powers, not hastily or impetuously, but gently and seriously. For, as in some law courts, the criers make more noise in

> 66 *The best cure for anger is to make immediate reparation in meekness; for, as the proverb says, fresh wounds are always the easiest to heal.* 99

their efforts to preserve quiet than would be made by those they seek to still, so, if we are impetuous in our attempts to restrain our anger, we cause greater discomposure in our hearts than before; and once thrown off its balance, the heart is no longer its own master.

Having then sought calmly to control yourself, follow the counsel given by St. Augustine in his old age to the young Bishop Auxilius. "Do," he said, "as it becomes a man to do; if with David thou feelest that thy spirit is vexed within thee, make haste to cry, 'Have mercy on me, O Lord,' that He may stretch forth His right hand to moderate thine anger." When we feel ourselves stirred with passion, we must imitate the Apostles amidst the raging storm and tempest, and call upon God to help us; then He will bid our angry passions to be still, and great shall be our peace. But I would have you remember, that when we pray to be delivered from the anger with which we are struggling, we should pray gently and calmly, without excitement, and so with all the other remedies we may adopt against this evil.

Furthermore, as soon as you are conscious of having committed a hasty action, lose no time in repairing the error by an act of gentleness towards the person with whom you have been irritated. Just as the surest cure for lying is to unsay a falsehood as soon as we are conscious of having told it, so the best cure for anger is to make immediate reparation in meekness; for, as the proverb says, fresh wounds are always the easiest to heal.

Moreover, when you are at peace and without any cause for anger, try to lay in a stock of gentleness and meekness, always speaking and acting both in things great and small as gently as possible. And remember that the Spouse in the Canticle of Canticles had honey not only from her lips, but that it was "under her tongue," that is, in her breast; and she had not only honey but milk. (*Cant.* 4: 11). So we must not only use gentle words towards our neighbors, but must be filled with gentleness, that is, our very inmost soul. And we must not be satisfied

> **Canticle of Canticles**
>
> This book of the Hebrew Scriptures, also known as Song of Songs (or Song of Solomon), is an allegorical poem depicting the relationship between God (the Bridegroom of the narrative) and Israel (the Bride). In Christian understanding the lovers symbolize Christ and his Church.

with the aromatic fragrance of honey, that is, with agreeable and courteous dealings towards strangers, but we must have the milk of charity towards our own household, and not resemble those who are angels abroad and devils at home.

For Reflection

1. According to the reading, what are the two virtues that help perfect our attitude toward God and neighbor? What does Francis say are some indications that we have not genuinely developed these virtues?

2. Saint Francis writes, "We must oppose what is wrong . . . but we must do so quietly and gently." He then gives analogies to illustrate his point. Explain his analogy of the visiting prince in your own words. What might be a modern parallel?

3. Paraphrase what Saint Augustine says to Profuturus, as recalled by Saint Francis in this reading. Do you agree or disagree with the advice of Augustine and Francis regarding anger? Explain your response.

4. The excerpt concludes by reminding us to treat those closest to us with the courtesy we show to strangers. Why is it sometimes so difficult to be kind and loving to close friends and family? Why is it so necessary?

6 Saying Yes to God

Introduction

A frequently painted scene in Western art is the Annunciation—the event in which the Archangel Gabriel came to Mary to announce that she would become the mother of the Messiah. Saint Luke recounts Mary's response, a perfect yes: "Behold, I am the handmaid of the Lord. May it be done to me according to your word" (Luke 1:38).

What does it mean to be a follower of Christ? It means saying yes to God in many and varied ways throughout our day. By saying yes, Mary cooperated with God's plan. And we can cooperate with God today through our yes—our affirming thoughts, words, and actions. Mary of Nazareth, Patrick of Ireland, Francis of Assisi, and Ignatius of Loyola each said yes to God in their own ways. In this chapter you will read selections representing each of these great saints, who together span more than fifteen hundred years of the Church's history.

In the first reading, Luke tells us of the angel Gabriel's visit to Mary, a young Jewish woman living in Nazareth. Immediately following this monumental event, Mary visits her relative Elizabeth to share the good news of Jesus with others. In Mary's prayer of praise, which we call the *Magnificat*, she says, "My soul proclaims the greatness of the Lord; / my spirit rejoices in God my savior" (Luke 1:46). Mary's *Magnificat* has become a familiar and beloved canticle, or song, of praise and affirmation in the Church.

Moving ahead about four hundred years, you will read a selection by Saint Patrick, remembered as the Apostle of Ireland for his zeal in bringing the good news of Jesus to the Irish people. "St. Patrick's **Breastplate**" captures his sense of intimacy with Christ, whom he intensely experienced during his enslavement by Irish captors. In this prayer he says yes to Christ, inviting Christ to be with him and beside him through all of life's joys and sorrows. Through Christ, Patrick recognized that God is Three-in-One, a **Trinity** of loving persons. A legend even says that Patrick used the three leaves of a shamrock to teach his followers the truth of the Holy Trinity.

The third reading, the "Canticle of the Creatures," comes from Giovanni Francesco di Bernardone—better known to us as Saint Francis of Assisi. Francis enjoyed his social life as a wealthy merchant's son in twelfth-century Assisi. Then he was taken prisoner on a military expedition. After his release he was a different person, seeking solace in the countryside. It was near the leper colony outside Assisi that Francis heard God calling him. With all the zeal of his youth he embraced this calling to bring God's peace and love to the world. Francis said yes to God in his care for the poor and the lepers, his promotion of peace during the Crusades, his enchantment with all creatures, and his experience of God in all creation. He wrote the "Canticle of the Creatures" near the end of his life; the verse praising "Sister Bodily Death" was expressed on his deathbed. The canticle invites us to appreciate a created world that by its very nature says yes to God.

The final selections are two prayers attributed to a sixteenth-century Spanish saint, Ignatius of Loyola. He sought worldly glory as a knight on a European battlefield. While recovering from a cannonball wound, Ignatius asked a friend to bring him novels to pass the time. Instead, he received books on Christ and the saints. The story of Saint Francis of

breastplate Armor that covers and protects the chest from injury.

Trinity From the Latin *trinus*, meaning "threefold," referring to the central mystery of the Christian faith that God exists as a communion of three distinct and interrelated divine Persons: Father, Son, and Holy Spirit. The doctrine of the Trinity is a mystery that is inaccessible to human reason alone and is known through Divine Revelation only.

Assisi particularly captured his imagination. Through those stories the fire of God's love ignited his heart and transformed his aspirations into a desire to live "for the greater glory of God," now the motto of the Society of Jesus, or Jesuit order, which he founded. His best-known writing is the **Spiritual Exercises**, which begins with the prayer *"Anima Christi"* (Latin for "soul of Christ") and concludes with the *"Suscipe"* (Latin for "receive"). Both prayers, through Saint Ignatius's yes, set us an example of complete trust and total abandonment to the will of God.

Luke 1:26–38,40–55

The angel Gabriel was sent from God to a town of Galilee called Nazareth, to a virgin betrothed to a man named Joseph, of the house of David, and the virgin's name was Mary. And coming to her, he said, "Hail, favored one! The Lord is with you." But she was greatly troubled at what was said and pondered what sort of greeting this might be. Then the angel said to her, "Do not be afraid, Mary, for you have found favor with God. Behold, you will conceive in your womb and bear a son, and you shall name him Jesus. He will be great and will be called Son of the Most High, and the Lord God will give him the throne of David his father, and he will rule over the house of Jacob forever, and of his kingdom there will be no end." But Mary said to the angel, "How can this be, since I have no relations with a man?" And the angel said to her in

The Hail Mary

The Hail Mary, sometimes called by its Latin title, *Ave Maria*, combines two passages from the Gospel of Luke: the Angel Gabriel's salutation to Mary at the Annunciation, "Hail favored one! The Lord is with you" (1:28); and Elizabeth's greeting at the Visitation, "Most blessed are you among women, and blessed is the fruit of your womb" (1:42).

reply, "The holy Spirit will come upon you, and the power of the Most High will overshadow you.

Therefore the child to be born will be called holy, the Son of God. And behold, Elizabeth, your rela-

> 66 *May it be done to me according to your word.* 99

tive, has also conceived a son in her old age, and this is the sixth month for her who was called barren; for nothing will be impossible for God." Mary said, "Behold, I am the handmaid of the Lord. May it be done to me according to your word." . . .

. . . She entered the house of Zechariah and greeted Elizabeth. When Elizabeth heard Mary's greeting, the infant leaped in her womb, and Elizabeth, filled with the holy Spirit, cried out in a loud voice and said, "Most blessed are you among women, and blessed is the fruit of your womb. And how does this happen to me that the mother of my Lord should come to me? For at the moment the sound of your greeting reached my ears, the infant in my womb leaped for joy. Blessed are you who believed that what was spoken to you by the Lord would be fulfilled." And Mary said:

> "My soul proclaims the greatness of the Lord;
>> my spirit rejoices in God my savior.
> For he has looked upon his handmaid's lowliness;
>> behold, from now on will all ages call me blessed.
> The Mighty One has done great things for me,
>> and holy is his name.
> His mercy is from age to age
>> to those who fear him.
> He has shown might with his arm,
>> dispersed the arrogant of mind and heart.
> He has thrown down the rulers from their thrones
>> but lifted up the lowly.
> The hungry he has filled with good things;

the rich he has sent away empty.

He has helped Israel his servant,

remembering his mercy,

according to his promise to our fathers,

to Abraham and to his descendants forever."

"Saint Patrick's Breastplate"

By Saint Patrick

I bind to myself today
The strong virtue of the Invocation of the Trinity:
I believe the Trinity in the Unity
The Creator of the Universe.
I bind to myself today
The virtue of the Incarnation of Christ with His Baptism,
The virtue of His crucifixion with His burial,
The virtue of His Resurrection with His Ascension,
The virtue of His coming on the Judgement Day.

I bind to myself today
The virtue of the love of seraphim,
In the obedience of angels,
In the hope of resurrection unto reward,
In prayers of Patriarchs,
In predictions of Prophets,
In preaching of Apostles,
In faith of Confessors,
In purity of holy Virgins,
In deeds of righteous men.

I bind to myself today
The power of Heaven,
The light of the sun,

The brightness of the moon,
The splendour of fire,
The flashing of lightning,
The swiftness of wind,
The depth of sea,
The stability of earth,
The compactness of rocks.

I bind to myself today
God's Power to guide me,
God's Might to uphold me,
God's Wisdom to teach me,
God's Eye to watch over me,
God's Ear to hear me,
God's Word to give me speech,
God's Hand to guide me,
God's Way to lie before me,
God's Shield to shelter me,
God's Host to secure me,
Against the snares of demons,
Against the seductions of vices,
Against the lusts of nature,
Against everyone who meditates injury to me,
Whether far or near,
Whether few or with many.

I invoke today all these virtues
Against every hostile merciless power
Which may assail my body and my soul,
Against the incantations of false prophets,
Against the black laws of heathenism,
Against the false laws of heresy,
Against the deceits of idolatry . . .
Against every knowledge that binds the soul of man.

Christ, protect me today
Against every poison, against burning,
Against drowning, against death-wound,
That I may receive abundant reward.

Christ with me, Christ before me,
Christ behind me, Christ within me,
Christ beneath me, Christ above me,
Christ at my right, Christ at my left,
Christ in the fort,
Christ in the chariot seat, . . .
Christ in the heart of everyone who thinks of me,
Christ in the mouth of everyone who speaks to me,
Christ in every eye that sees me,
Christ in every ear that hears me.

I bind to myself today
The strong virtue of an invocation of the Trinity,
I believe the Trinity in the Unity
The Creator of the Universe.

"Canticle of the Creatures"
By Saint Francis of Assisi

Most High, all-powerful, good Lord,
Yours are the praises, the glory, the honor, and all blessing (see Rev 4:9,11).
To You alone, Most High, do they belong,
and no man is worthy to mention Your name.
Praised be You, my Lord, with all your creatures,
especially Sir Brother Sun,
Who is the day and through whom You give us light.
And he is beautiful and radiant with great splendor;
and bears a likeness of You, Most High One.

Praised be You, my Lord, through Sister Moon and the stars,
in heaven You formed them clear and precious and beautiful.
Praised be You, my Lord, through Brother Wind,
and through the air, cloudy and serene, and every kind of weather
through which You give sustenance to Your creatures.
Praised be You, my Lord, through Sister Water,
which is very useful and humble and precious and chaste.
Praised be You, my Lord, through Brother Fire,
through whom You light the night
and he is beautiful and playful and robust and strong.
Praised be You, my Lord, through our Sister Mother Earth,
who sustains and governs us,
and who produces varied fruits with colored flowers and herbs.
Praised be You, my Lord, through those who give pardon for Your love[1]
and bear infirmity and tribulation.
Blessed are those who endure in peace
for by You, Most High, they shall be crowned.
Praised be You, my Lord, through our Sister Bodily Death,[2]
from whom no living man can escape.
Woe to those who die in mortal sin.
Blessed are those whom death will find in Your most holy will,
for the second death shall do them no harm (see Rev 2:11; 20:6).
Praise and bless my Lord and give Him thanks
and serve Him with great humility.

Endnotes

1. The second section of the Canticle begins with this stanza. Since the human person is not part of the chorus of the previous section, he now enters into the hymn through an identification with the God-man, Jesus Christ, i.e., by suffering weakness and tribulation, pardoning out of love, and enduring in peace.
2. The third section begins with this stanza.

"*Anima Christi*" and "*Suscipe*," from the *Spiritual Exercises*

By Saint Ignatius of Loyola

Anima Christi

Soul of Christ, sanctify me.
Body of Christ, save me.
Blood of Christ, inebriate me.
Water from the side of Christ, wash me.
Passion of Christ, strengthen me.
O Good Jesus, hear me.
Within your wounds hide me.
Permit me not to be separated from you.
From the wicked foe, defend me.
At the hour of my death, call me.

Suscipe

Take, Lord, all my liberty.
Receive my memory, my intellect, and will.
Whatever I have or hold you have given to me;
so I return them to you to be used according to your will.
Give us only your love and your grace,
and with these we are rich enough and ask for nothing more.

For Reflection

1. In the Visitation narrative from the Gospel of Luke, how did the child in Elizabeth's womb respond to Mary's visit? What do you think Luke wants us to understand about this response?

2. Why is Patrick's prayer called a "breastplate"? Following Patrick's example, write your own breastplate prayer in either a short paragraph or an eight-line poem.

3. To what elements of nature does Saint Francis of Assisi assign human characteristics? How does humanizing natural elements change how we think of them?

4. We still use the Latin names of the prayers by Saint Ignatius. Based on your reading of these prayers, write a new English title describing each (not a direct translation). For each prayer, give the new title and explain how it fits the text.

Part 2
The Law of Love Revealed

7   What Should I Do?

Introduction

You are nervous about an upcoming midterm in your most difficult class. Then a few classmates ask you to join them in cheating on the test. What should you do?

Making decisions is the nature of human life, and some of our hardest decisions involve ethics or morals. In the following excerpt from *Making Disciples: A Handbook of Christian Moral Formation*, Timothy O'Connell posits a basic human question, What should I do?, and then explores a response that draws on biblical **values**. O'Connell teaches values and **ethics** as a professor at Loyola University Chicago. In the classroom as well as in his many books, public lectures, and radio and TV appearances, he explores how we can face ethical challenges by living a value-based life and by sharing values with others. In particular, as a specialist in Christian ethics, he examines how our

values The standards and principles by which decisions are made. Different types of values include personal values, cultural or societal values, aesthetic values, and in the case of this chapter, moral and ethical values.

ethics The principles that guide moral behavior. Christian ethics is informed by biblical values and those taught by Jesus and his Church.

Tradition From the Latin meaning "to hand on"; refers to the process of passing on the Gospel message. Tradition, which began with the oral communication of the Gospel by the Apostles, was written down in the Scriptures, is handed down and lived out in the life of the Church, and is interpreted by the Magisterium under the guidance of the Holy Spirit.

relationship with Christ informs our system of values, which in turn guides how we respond to life's moral questions.

The ultimate value that we embrace as Christians is to live a new life in Christ—a life of love. God has revealed this value through the divine law written on our hearts and through Scripture and **Tradition**. He revealed it most fully by sending his only Son, Jesus Christ. Our morality is therefore guided by this ultimate value. Jesus not only teaches us God's law for living rightly and morally, but he actually makes it possible for us to live this new life.

O'Connell explores Christian morality in this excerpt by recalling the Gospel narrative in which a lawyer asks Jesus how to achieve eternal life. When Jesus turns the question back to the inquirer, the lawyer's response reflects the moral values of Judaism. O'Connell reminds us that Jesus expands on these values by telling the Parable of the Good Samaritan. This story expresses the universality of God's command to love, the ultimate Christian value.

The law of God's love is inscribed upon our hearts—"is built into the fabric of humanity," as O'Connell says (p. 10). When we follow the law of love to respond to the moral questions of our lives, we genuinely live a new life in Christ.

Excerpt from *Making Disciples: A Handbook of Christian Moral Formation*

By Timothy E. O'Connell

Morality: Human Life Lived Humanely

Sometimes, when one hears people discussing morality, one gets the impression that this reality is something imposed on human persons from the outside. That is, there is an implied presumption that morality is the enemy, beleaguering and burdening me. The suggestion is that if certain people would just stop imposing their demands on me, be that person God, society, or my parents, I could move on with my life without the burden of morality. Then, at last, I could be happy and well adjusted, free at last of the arbitrary demands of these unforgiving voices!

Yet a bit of reflection on our own experience shows that this is not true. The human question What should I do? is an unavoidable part of everyday life. It is a question asked by every human person, unless that person is subject to some sort of serious pathology. It is a question that no normal, mature person can ever avoid.

But let's be clear about the question. What should I do? is a question that can be asked at several different levels. The question can be asked at a "technical" or "procedural" level, with no reference to anything really substantial. That is, we can inquire about how to move most efficiently from here to there, without ever inquiring about whether moving from here to there is worth doing at all. We can wonder how to get the job, how to make the money, how to convince the other person to become intimate, how to conquer the enemy. We can simply take as given that these are worthy objectives for life and then inquire about how best to achieve them. And often enough we do ask this question in that technical way.

But that is not how the question is being understood here. The question What should I do? can also be asked at a deeper level. We can ask: What is the right thing to do? What is the sort of thing a human being ought to do? That is the question we are discussing, and the point being made here is that this deeper, more fundamental question is also a question asked by every normal, mature human being. Sooner or later, people always seem to come to that question. It is not imposed on them from the outside; on the contrary, it seems to arise from the nature of being human.

This does not mean that people always answer the question well. They may answer the question thoughtfully or cavalierly. They may answer it insightfully or naively. Their answers may be distorted by prejudice or ignorance, may be hobbled by pressures of time or limitations of circumstance. But as best I can tell, human persons inevitably ask it.

Consequently, morality is not imposed from the outside, in some arbitrary, posterior, after-the-fact manner. On the contrary, it is built into the fabric of humanity. If all those outside voices were someday to leave us alone, the voice of morality (what is traditionally called the voice of conscience) would be with us still. For the voice is the voice of oneself.

But that is not all; a further point must be made. We human beings are very diverse. We come in various races, various cultures, and two genders. We have greatly diverse views of what life is all about and of what it finally means to be human. So when we ask the question What should I do? we ask it in many different ways. We ask it, indeed, in our own way and in light of who we really are.

> *Morality is not imposed from the outside, in some arbitrary, posterior, after-the-fact manner. On the contrary, it is built into the fabric of humanity.*

Consequently, as the question is actually formulated by particular persons, so it is formulated in necessarily diverse ways.

If, for example, I have faith in God, if I believe that God's love has brought me into existence and carries me through every day, then my question will reflect that fact. My question will be: Given God's love for me, what should I do? And if, going further, I have faith in Jesus, if I believe that Jesus Christ is the presence of God in this world, the gift of God to this world, and the one whose loving sacrifice brings us home, then my question will change again. My question will be: Given God and God's gift in Jesus, what should I do?

Christian Morality

This last question, then, brings us to the phenomenon of Christian morality. For Christian morality is nothing more or less than the answer given by Christian persons as they respond to the unavoidable human question in the unavoidably Christian formulation that they give it in their everyday lives. It is the answer given by people who believe in Jesus, as they reflect on their lives, understand those lives in light of the person and deeds of Jesus, and then seek to discern how they ought to act.

In answering their question, however, it is no surprise that Christians depend not only on their experience and their autonomous reflection but also on the words of Jesus. For example, consider the following:

> Just then a lawyer stood up to test Jesus. "Teacher," he said, "what must I do to inherit eternal life?" He said to him, "What is written in the law? What do you read there?" He answered, "You shall love the Lord your God with all your

heart, and with all your soul, and with all your strength, and with all your mind; and your neighbor as yourself." And he said to him, "You have given the right answer; do this and you will live." (Luke 19:10–28)[1]

Perhaps no text is more frequently cited in articulating the answer proposed by Christian morality than this. But for that reason, it is worth pointing out that it is a particularly interesting text. Indeed, in a couple of different regards it deserves to be explored.

First of all, it is worth noting that, although the text is usually presented because it is presumed to express *Jesus'* personal "take" on morality, in the text it is not Jesus who gives the answer. It is the lawyer. So at the very least, one must oddly comment that the classic summary of Jesus' view of morality expresses a view that Jesus receives from another, a view he does not articulate but merely affirms.

But if this situation is somehow odd, it is also quite understandable. For, as scholars explain to us, Jesus is not inquiring simplistically into the personal whims of the lawyer. Rather, he is probing in order to assess the lawyer's education. It seems that the answer offered by the lawyer is not, after all, a particularly innovative answer. On the contrary, it is an answer already well accepted in his Jewish community. The "two great commandments," as they are called, are both found in the Hebrew scriptures (Deut. 6:5 and Lev. 19:18); they are not something new with Jesus at all. And, what is more, for generations it had been widely accepted in Jewish culture that all of the commandments of God, and that most traditional of summaries of God's commandments known as the Ten Commandments, could themselves be summarized in the two great

Love God and Neighbor

The Two Great Commandments that Jesus taught have their origins in the Pentateuch, also called the Law of Moses. The first great command is found in the Book of Deuteronomy in its Shema prayer: "Hear, O Israel! The LORD is our God, the LORD alone! Therefore, you shall love the LORD, your God, with your whole heart, and with your whole being, and with your whole strength" (6:4–5). The second command, "You shall love your neighbor as yourself," is found in the Book of Leviticus (19:18).

commandments: love God and love your neighbor. So in this text, once the lawyer asks Jesus what he must do to inherit eternal life (a question that was perhaps manipulative from the start), Jesus responds with his own question: "Don't you know the commonly accepted answer to the question?" Then the lawyer saves himself by showing that he does, indeed, know that answer: love God and neighbor. Jesus then does nothing more than embrace this tradition and commend it to the lawyer and his other listeners.

So much for distinctively Christian ethics, for a distinctively Christian response to the inevitable human question! Still, if we probe more deeply, this text from Luke is not without innovation. In the following verses the lawyer, "to justify himself," seeks to clarify who the neighbor might be, and Jesus responds with the famous story of the Good Samaritan. That is, in Jesus' view being a neighbor is not a matter of having a relationship or being part of one's group. Quite the contrary, being a neighbor is an attitude of life that should manifest itself in all human encounters.

In this text, and in many others, then, Jesus does articulate something like a characteristically Christian response to the inevitable human question. And what is that response? It is the universalization of the love command.

Endnote

1. Pope John Paul II uses this text, in its Matthean version (19:16–22), as the basis for a meditation on the nature of morality; see "Veritatis Splendor," *Origins* 23:18 (October 14, 1993): §§6–27.

For Reflection

1. According to O'Connell, what moral question do we inevitably ask ourselves? Why is it inevitable? What does he say are the different levels at which we can ask that question?

2. In your own words, summarize the passage that O'Connell says is most frequently cited to explain Christian morality. What is Jesus' take on the moral question in that passage?

3. The author says that "being a neighbor is an attitude of life that should manifest itself in all human encounters." What does it mean to be a neighbor, and why is it important in all of our interactions? Give an example of how you can be a neighbor to someone in your life today.

8 Naming Our Idols, Claiming Our Heroes

Introduction

If you ever visit the University of Illinois at Urbana-Champaign, be sure to stop by Saint John's Catholic Newman Center, the largest Newman Center in the United States. Throughout the world, Newman Centers are beacons of Christ's light, providing campus ministry programs to serve the spiritual, social, and scholastic needs of Catholic students at secular colleges and universities. Newman Centers are named in honor of Blessed John Henry Newman, the brilliant nineteenth-century Oxford University scholar and priest in the Church of England who converted to Catholicism, was later made a cardinal, and wrote compellingly of the intersection of faith and reason.

Newman was a man of deep intellect and even deeper convictions. His motto was *cor ad cor loquitur*—heart speaks to heart. In the poem you will read first in this chapter, God's heart speaks to Newman's heart. Newman wrote this short piece at sea, while sailing from Italy back to England soon after a life-threatening illness. Originally called "The Pillar of the Cloud," the poem was later set to music and titled "Lead, Kindly Light." In this poem Newman acknowl-

> ### Nineteenth-Century England
>
> John Henry Newman is writing in nineteenth-century industrialized England. A few years before Newman wrote "Saintliness the Standard of Christian Principle," Charles Dickens wrote *A Christmas Carol*. You may know that story as a holiday tale, but Dickens also meant it as a social commentary on the poverty that plagued London. The attitude of Ebenezer Scrooge, before his ghostly visits, is a good example of what Newman calls the "moral effects of an eclipsed sun."

edges the "encircling gloom" that any of us can experience and contrasts a life of seeking our own way with a life spent following the light of God's grace day by day.

In his other writings, Newman examined how God's light is revealed in models of saintliness. God leads us, according to Newman, through the good example set by those whose hearts can speak to the heart and conscience of another. The second selection in this chapter is from a discourse in which Newman contrasts sanctity with idolatry, specifically the value we place on worldly concerns. Though written more than 160 years ago, his social commentary still rings true when we look at the messages of the media today and the influence they have on our values.

Newman's writings challenge us not to allow false idols to block the light of Christ. Instead he defines saintliness and summons us to claim these heroes and seek their guidance in living a moral life.

"The Pillar of the Cloud (Lead, Kindly Light)"
By Blessed John Henry Newman

Lead, Kindly Light, amid the encircling gloom,
    Lead Thou me on!
The night is dark, and I am far from home—
    Lead Thou me on!
Keep Thou my feet; I do not ask to see
The distant scene—one step enough for me.
I was not ever thus, nor pray'd that Thou
    Shouldst lead me on.
I loved to choose and see my path; but now,
    Lead Thou me on!
I loved the garish day, and, spite of fears,
Pride ruled my will: remember not past years.

So long Thy power hath blessed me, sure it still
    Will lead me on,
O'er moor and fen, o'er crag and torrent, till
    The night is gone;
And with the morn those angel faces smile
Which I have loved long since, and lost awhile.

At Sea.
June 16, 1833.

Excerpt from Discourse 5, "Saintliness the Standard of Christian Principle"

By Blessed John Henry Newman

In the breast of every one there dwells a feeling or perception, which tells him the difference between right and wrong, and is the standard by which to measure thoughts and actions. It is called conscience; and even though it be not at all times powerful enough to rule us, still it is distinct and decisive enough to influence our views and form our judgments in the various matters which come before us. Yet even this office it cannot perform adequately without external assistance; it needs to be regulated and sustained. Left to itself, though it tells truly at first, it soon becomes wavering, ambiguous, and false; it needs good teachers and good examples to keep it up to the mark and line of duty; and the misery is, that these external helps, teachers, and examples are in many instances **wanting**.

Nay, to the great multitude of men they are so far wanting, that conscience loses its way and guides the soul in its journey heavenward but indirectly and circuitously. . . . I say, it is a most miserable and frightful thought, that, in this country, among this people which boasts that it is so Christian and so enlightened, the sun in the heavens is so eclipsed that the mirror of conscience can catch and reflect few rays, and serves but poorly and scantily to preserve the foot from error. That inward light, given as it is by God, is powerless to illuminate the horizon, to mark out for us our direction, and to comfort us with the certainty that we are making for our Eternal Home. That light was intended to set up within us a standard of right and of truth; to tell us our duty on every emergency, to instruct us in detail what sin is, to judge between all things which come before us, to discriminate the precious from the vile, to hinder us from being seduced by what is pleasant and agreeable, and to dissipate the **sophisms** of our reason. But alas! what ideas of truth, what ideas of holiness, what ideas of heroism, what ideas of the good and great, have the multitude of men? . . .

Look around, my brethren, and answer for yourselves. Contemplate the objects of this people's praise, survey their standards, ponder their ideas and judgments, and then tell me whether it is not most evident, from their very notion of the desirable and the excellent, that greatness, and goodness, and sanctity, and sublimity, and truth are unknown to them;

> 66 *What ideas of truth, what ideas of holiness, what ideas of heroism, what ideas of the good and great, have the multitude of men?* 99

and that they not only do not pursue, but do not even admire, those high attributes of the Divine Nature. *This* is what I am insisting on, not what they actually do or what they are, but what they revere, what they adore, what their gods are. Their god is **mammon**; I do not mean to say that all seek to be wealthy, but that all bow down before wealth. Wealth is that to which the multitude of men pay an instinctive homage. They measure happiness by wealth; and by wealth they measure respectability. Numbers, I say, there are who never dream that they shall ever be rich themselves, but who still at the sight of wealth feel an involuntary reverence and awe, just as if a rich man must be a good man. They like to be noticed by some particular rich man; they like on some occasion to have spoken with him; they like to know those who know him, to be intimate with his dependants, to have entered his house, nay, to know him by sight. Not, I repeat, that it ever comes into their mind that the like wealth will one day be theirs; not that they *see* the wealth,

wanting Lacking; not found.

sophisms Arguments used to deceive. "Sophisms of reason" include ways of wrongly justifying a thought, word, or action.

mammon Biblical reference to wealth and greed; see Matthew 6:24.

for the man who has it may dress, and live, and look like other men; not
that they expect to gain some benefit from it: no, theirs is a disinterested
homage, it is a homage resulting from an honest, genuine, hearty admira-
tion of wealth for its own sake, such as that pure love which holy men
feel for the Maker of all; it is a homage resulting from a profound faith in
wealth, from the intimate sentiment of their hearts, that, however a man
may look,—poor, mean, starved, decrepit, vulgar; or again, though he may
be ignorant, or diseased, or feeble-minded, though he have the character
of being a tyrant or a profligate, yet, if he be rich, he differs from all others; if he be rich, he has a gift, a spell, an omnipotence;—that with wealth
he may do all things.

Wealth is one idol of the day, and notoriety is a second. I am not
speaking, I repeat, of what men actually pursue, but of what they look up
to, what they revere. Men may not have the opportunity of pursuing what
they admire still. Never could notoriety exist as it does now, in any former
age of the world; now that the news of the hour from all parts of the
world, private news as well as public, is brought day by day to every individual, as I may say, of the community, to the poorest artisan and the most
secluded peasant, by processes so uniform, so unvarying, so spontaneous,
that they almost bear the semblance of a natural law. And hence notoriety,
or the making a noise in the world, has come to be considered a great
good in itself, and a ground of veneration. Time was when men could
only make a display by means of expenditure; and the world used to gaze
with wonder on those who had large establishments, many servants, many
horses, richly-furnished houses, gardens, and parks: it does so still, that
is, when it has the opportunity of doing so: for such magnificence is the
fortune of the few, and comparatively few are its witnesses. Notoriety, or,
as it may be called, newspaper fame, is to the many what style and fashion,
to use the language of the world, are to those who are within or belong
to the higher circles; it becomes to them a sort of idol, worshipped for its
own sake, and without any reference to the shape in which it comes before
them. It may be an evil fame or a good fame; it may be the notoriety of
a great statesman, or of a great preacher, or of a great speculator, or of a
great experimentalist, or of a great criminal; of one who has laboured in
the improvement of our schools, or hospitals, or prisons, or workhouses,

or of one who has robbed his neighbour of his wife. It matters not; so that a man is talked much of, and read much of, he is thought much of; nay, let him even have died justly under the hands of the law, still he will be made a sort of martyr of. . . . For the question with men is, not whether he is great, or good, or wise, or holy; not whether he is base, and vile, and odious, but whether he is in the mouths of men, whether he has centred on himself the attention of many, whether he has done something out of the way, whether he has been (as it were) canonised in the publications of the hour. . . .

. . . Still consider only what a change there will be in its [society's] views and estimation of things, as soon as it has heard and has faith in the word of God, as soon as it understands that wealth, and notoriety, and influence, and high place, are not the first of blessings and the real standard of good; but that saintliness and all its attendants,—saintly purity, saintly poverty, heroic fortitude and patience, self-sacrifice for the sake of others, renouncement of the world, the favour of Heaven, the protection of Angels, the smile of the Blessed Virgin, the gifts of grace, the interpositions of miracle, the intercommunion of merits,—that these are the high and precious things, the things to be looked up to, the things to be reverently spoken of. . . .

. . . Very various are the Saints, their very variety is a token of God's workmanship; but however various, and whatever was their special line of duty, they have been heroes in it; they have attained such noble self-command, they have so crucified the flesh, they have so renounced the world; they are so meek, so gentle, so tender-hearted, so merciful, so sweet, so cheerful, so full of prayer, so diligent, so forget-

> **Blessed John Henry Newman (1801–1890)**
>
> At the Mass for Newman's beatification in 2010, Pope Benedict XVI declared, "The definite service to which Blessed John Henry was called involved applying his keen intellect and his prolific pen to many of the most pressing 'subjects of the day.'" The Pope continued, "I would like to pay particular tribute to his vision for education, which has done so much to shape the ethos that is the driving force behind Catholic schools and colleges today." Blessed John Henry Newman's feast day is October 9.

ful of injuries; they have sustained such great and continued pains, they have persevered in such vast labours, they have made such valiant confessions, they have wrought such abundant miracles, they have been blessed with such strange successes, that they have been the means of setting up a standard before us of truth, of magnanimity, of holiness, of love. They are not always our examples, we are not always bound to follow them; not more than we are bound to obey literally some of our Lord's precepts, such as turning the cheek or giving away the coat; not more than we can follow the course of the sun, moon, or stars in the heavens; but, though not always our examples, they are always our standard of right and good; they are raised up to be monuments and lessons, they remind us of God, they introduce us into the unseen world, they teach us what Christ loves, they track out for us the way which leads heavenward.

For Reflection

1. Based on both readings, what or who is Newman's "Kindly Light," and what help does he seek? Recall a time when you experienced an "encircling gloom." Who or what was your kindly light?

2. In the second reading, how does Newman describe conscience? What does he say our conscience requires so it can guide us effectively? Why are those conditions necessary?

3. In this reading Newman examines the metaphor of an eclipsed sun. What moral lesson does he illustrate with this metaphor? How can we apply this lesson to our culture today? Give one or two examples.

4. According to Newman, the people of his time revered two idols, even if they did not personally pursue them. What two idols does he identify? Describe a modern-day example of each idol.

9 Honoring Your Family, All for Jesus

Introduction

While making the 1969 BBC documentary *Something Beautiful for God*, about Mother Teresa of Calcutta, journalist Malcolm Muggeridge told his crew to record some footage in the Missionaries of Charity's Calcutta Home for the Dying in India. As Muggeridge later described in his book on Mother Teresa, also titled *Something Beautiful for God,* the lighting was inadequate; but the cameraman filmed a short segment anyway, not expecting to be able to use it. To everyone's surprise, the images that appeared on film were surrounded by a soft light. Muggeridge and his film crew considered this footage a photographic miracle.

Few people who met Mother Teresa were untouched by her holiness, for she responded to God's call to bring light to a world in darkness. She and her religious sisters in the Missionaries of Charity had been working in obscurity in the slums of Calcutta for eighteen years when Muggeridge filmed his documentary, which introduced Mother Teresa to the world. In 1979 she received the Nobel Peace Prize for her humanitarian work. Her extraordinary works of love for the destitute and dying were accompanied by her advocacy for ordinary works of love done in the name of Jesus. In her writings and public speeches, even

> **Missionaries of Charity**
>
> The Missionaries of Charity were established in 1950 by Mother Teresa to humbly serve the poorest of the poor of Calcutta, India. The founding community of twelve religious sisters has grown to more than four thousand worldwide who bring Christ's light and love to abandoned children, refugees, the elderly, victims of HIV/AIDS, and others who are sick or suffering.

just in conversation, she was often known to say, "All for Jesus!" That was how she lived, all for Jesus. And whether she was speaking to world leaders or college students, her message was always sincere and simple: Love, honor, and serve Jesus through the people in your life.

In the reading in this chapter, from her book *Words to Love By . . .* , Mother Teresa reminds us that the call to love, honor, and serve Jesus Christ and our fellow human beings begins in the family. "Whatever you do in your family"—for father or mother, sister or brother, daughter or son—"you do for Jesus," she says (p. 52). The law of God in the **Ten Commandments** teaches us to honor our father and mother, but that moral duty extends into the entire family. We honor our parents through our respect for them and for our family as a whole. And a family that loves and honors each other loves and honors God, as Mother Teresa illustrates in the stories here.

Mother Teresa—now Blessed Teresa of Calcutta, after her 2003 beatification—reminds us that we are created in the image of God, a divine Trinity of love. And "love begins at home," she says (p. 54). After all, she points out, if we cannot love those closest to us, how can we sincerely love others? How can we love God?

Ten Commandments Sometimes called the Decalogue, the list of ten norms, or rules of moral behavior, that God gave Moses and that are the basis of ethical conduct. The Fourth Commandment teaches us to honor our father and mother.

Excerpt from *Words to Love By* . . .

By Blessed Teresa of Calcutta

The best and surest way to learn the love of Jesus is through the family.

We are created in the image of God
　　　　in the image of Jesus as a human being.
Every child has been created for a greater thing
　　　　—to love and be loved.
From the very beginning
from the time there is life
from the time there is conception
there is the life of God
　　　　—the life of the living God.
That is why it is so wrong to destroy life
　　　　—to destroy the image of God.

Whatever you do in your family
　　　　for your children
　　　　for your husband
　　　　for your wife
　　you do for Jesus.

Many of the troubles of modern society are caused by broken families.
Many mothers and fathers are so busy that they are never home.
　　Children come home from school and there is no one
　　　　to receive them
　　　　to pay attention to them
　　　　to encourage them if they are sad
　　　　to share their joy if they are happy.
　　Children long for somebody
　　　　to accept them
　　　　to love them
　　　　to praise them
　　　　to be proud of them.

If they do not have this, they will go to the streets where there are plenty of people ready to accept them. The child can be lost. Much hatred and destruction is caused when a child is lost to the family.

Like our Lady and St. Joseph we must go and search for the child. When Jesus was lost they went and searched. They did not sit and wait. They did not rest until they found him.

We must bring the child back, make the child feel wanted.

Without the child there is no hope.

Love begins at home.
If we do not love one another who we see 24 hours
    how can we love those we see only once?
We show love by thoughtfulness
        by kindness
        by sharing joy
        by sharing a smile . . .
Through the little things.

A little child has no difficulty in loving
        has no obstacles to love.
And that is why Jesus said,
    "Unless you become like little children. . . ."

Once a lady came to me in great sorrow and told me that her daughter had lost her husband and a child. All the daughter's hatreds had turned on the mother. She wouldn't even see the mother.

So I said, "Now you think a bit about the little things that your daughter liked when she was a child. Maybe flowers or a special food. Try to give her some of these things without looking for a return."

And she started doing some of these things, like putting the daughter's favorite flower on the table, or leaving a beautiful piece of cloth for her. And she did not look for a return from the daughter.

Several days later the daughter said, "Mommy, come. I love you. I want you."

It was very beautiful.

By being reminded of the joy of childhood, the daughter recon-

nected with her family life.
She must have had a happy
childhood to go back to the
joy and happiness of her
mother's love.

communist Someone who believes that all property should be communal and distributed equally, not privately owned. Some interpretations of communism reject the idea of God or religion.

It is very important for
children to hear their parents talk about God. The children must be able to
ask about God.

Once I gave a prayer to a **communist** and he took it back to his family
and the children started to pray.

When he saw me again he said, "Mother, you don't know how your
prayer and picture have disturbed the whole family. The children want to
know who God is. They want to know why Mother is speaking this way."

The children are hungry.

That is why we need to pray together.

If the parent sets the example, the children will not forget how to pray
    how they love each other
    how they share sorrow
    how they share joy.
Children watch . . . they watch
    and they grow with that.

They will learn that it makes a difference how they live their lives by
watching what the parents do.

If we can bring prayer into the family, the family will stay together. They
will love one another. Just get together for five minutes.

Start with the Our Father, that's all!

Or we can say
    "My Lord I love you
    my God I am sorry
    my God I believe in you
    my God I trust you.
    Help us to love one another
    as you love us."

That is where your strength will come from when you teach each other in prayer.

God has sent the family—together as husband and wife and children—to be his love.

I once picked up a child of six or seven in the street and took her to Shishu Bhavin (a children's home) and gave her a bath, some clothes and some nice food. That evening the child ran away.

> 66 **God has sent the family—together as husband and wife and children—to be his love.** 99

We took the child in a second and a third time, and she ran away.

After the third time I sent a sister to follow her. The sister found the child sitting with her mother and sister under a tree. There was a little dish there and the mother was cooking food she had picked up from the streets.

They were cooking there

they were eating there

they were sleeping there.

It was their home.

And then we understood why the child ran away. The mother just loved that child. And the child loved the mother. They were so beautiful to each other.

The child said "*bari jabo*"—it was her home.

Her mother was her home.

Many factors in the industrial world suffocate the joy of loving. People have too much and they want more. They are discontent.

A family in Australia with six or seven children talked together and decided not to buy a new television. They wanted to enjoy each other more completely. They had enough of what they needed for each other in each other.

Instead of buying the television, they gave the money to me to do something for the poor Aborigines there.

They overcame something they thought divided them, an obstacle to the joy of loving.

And they recognized the sharing
            the talking
            the laughing
            the loving
            the teasing.
The whole family is simply delighted.

We have hundreds of American and European young people coming here to join the Hindus. They are looking for something.

I always ask them if "Jesus is not enough for you?"

We have to try to give Jesus to our youth. They must be able to look up and see Jesus. And they must be able to see him in the home.

For Reflection

1. According to Mother Teresa, where does love begin? What does she say are some ways that we can show love? Choose one of the ways she mentions, and tell about a concrete example from your own life.

2. Mother Teresa tells a story about a daughter's anger toward her mother. What really helped the daughter reconnect with her family, and why? What can we learn from this about how to love one another?

3. According to this reading, how can the modern, industrialized world lead us to forget the joy of loving? Do you agree or disagree? Explain your response.

10 The Seamless Garment of Life

Introduction

The oldest city in Germany is Trier, a former Roman fortification where Emperor Constantine experienced a great vision of victory through Christ. The Cathedral of Trier houses the tunic Jesus wore during his trial before the Crucifixion. The Gospel of John describes this robe in the Crucifixion narrative. When the Roman soldiers divided the clothes of Jesus among themselves, John explains, "they also took his tunic, but the tunic was seamless, woven in one piece from the top down. So they said to one another, 'Let's not tear it, but cast lots for it to see whose it will be'" (19:23–24). One tradition says that Christ's seamless tunic made its way to Trier through the mother of Constantine, Saint Helena.

This religious artifact, the seamless garment of Christ, is an image that Joseph Cardinal Bernardin introduces in his teaching about a consistent ethic of life, one that addresses the sacredness of all the stages and conditions of life, from the moment of conception through natural death. As chair of the Committee on Pro-Life Activities of the **National Conference of Catholic Bishops** in the early 1990s, Bernardin sought to define and defend an all-encompassing moral vision that promotes respect for the sacredness of human life.

Human Rights

Human rights are basic, universal, natural rights to which all people are entitled. The Declaration of Independence considers the human rights to be "self-evident" and "unalienable," naming specific rights to life, liberty, and the pursuit of happiness. In Judeo-Christian teaching, human rights flow from the innate dignity of the human person created in the image of God.

The excerpt you will read here is from a lecture that Bernardin gave in 1984, titled "A Consistent Ethic of Life: Continuing the Dialogue." He covers three topics: his argument in favor of a consistent ethic of life; four levels of the issue, as he sees them; and the role that this ethic of life can play in the Church and in society. He addresses a range of human rights issues, from **abortion** to **euthanasia** to capital punishment. His argument for a consistent ethic of life is based on the understanding that although not all issues regarding respect for life are necessarily equivalent, all do have a common connection. Calling each of us to take a stand on at least one of these different but connected issues, Bernardin explores the fruitfulness of identifying and applying a singular principle to a diversity of life issues. He concludes by summoning the Church to be a public witness in promoting a consistent ethic of life.

National Conference of Catholic Bishops The former name of the United States Conference of Catholic Bishops. Each country or region has its own conference of bishops supporting the work of the Church in that part of the world.

abortion The deliberate termination of a pregnancy by killing the unborn child. It is a grave sin and a crime against human life.

euthanasia A direct action, or a deliberate lack of action, that causes the death of a person who is disabled, sick, or dying.

Although he was a tireless advocate for all issues involved in promoting a culture of life, Bernardin may be remembered most for the life-affirming way in which he coped with cancer, from which he died in 1996. He was known to stay for hours after many treatments, comforting other patients who were struggling to overcome cancer and were facing the prospect of death. The seamless garment of his own life was that of a champion who fought in a personal way to promote respect for human life from womb to tomb.

Excerpt from a Lecture, "A Consistent Ethic of Life: Continuing the Dialogue"

By Cardinal Joseph Bernardin

The Seamless Garment: The Logic of the Case

. . . The case for a consistent ethic of life—one which stands for the protection of the right to life and the promotion of the rights which enhance life from womb to tomb—manifests the positive potential of the Catholic moral and social tradition. It is both a complex and a demanding tradition; it joins the humanity of the unborn infant and the humanity of the hungry; it calls for positive legal action to prevent the killing of the unborn or the aged and positive societal action to provide shelter for the homeless and education for the illiterate. The potential of the moral and social vision is appreciated in a new way when the systemic vision of Catholic ethics is seen as the background for the specific positions we take on a range of issues.

> 66 *The case for a consistent ethic of life manifests the positive potential of the Catholic moral and social tradition.* 99

In response to those who fear otherwise, I contend that the systemic vision of a consistent ethic of life will not erode our crucial public opposition to the direction of the arms race; neither will it smother our persistent and necessary public opposition to abortion. The systemic vision is rooted in the conviction that our opposition to these distinct problems has a common foundation and that both Church and society are served by making it evident.

A consistent ethic of life does not equate the problem of taking life (e.g. through abortion and in war) with the problem of promoting human dignity (through humane programs of nutrition, health care, and housing). But a consistent ethic identifies both the protection of life and its promotion as moral questions. It argues for a continuum of life which must be sustained in the face of diverse and distinct threats.

A consistent ethic does not say everyone in the Church must do all things, but it does say that . . . the way we oppose one threat should be related to support for a systemic vision of life. It is not necessary or possible for every person to engage in each issue, but it is both possible and necessary for the Church as a whole to cultivate a conscious explicit connection among the several issues. And it is very necessary for preserving a systemic vision that individuals and groups who seek to witness to life at one point of the spectrum of life not be seen as insensitive to or even opposed to other moral claims on the overall spectrum of life. Consistency does rule out contradictory moral positions about the unique value of human life. No one is called to do everything, but each of us can do something. And we can strive not to stand against each other when the protection and the promotion of life are at stake.

The Seamless Garment: The Levels of the Question

A consistent ethic of life should honor the complexity of the multiple issues it must address. It is necessary to distinguish several levels of the question. Without attempting to be comprehensive, allow me to explore four distinct dimensions of a consistent ethic.

First, at the level of general moral principles, it is possible to identify a single principle with diverse applications. . . . I [have] used the prohibition against direct attacks on innocent life. This principle is both central to the Catholic moral vision and systematically related to a range of specific moral issues. It prohibits direct attacks on unborn life in the womb, direct attacks on civilians in warfare, and the direct killing of patients in nursing homes. Each of these topics has a constituency in society concerned with the morality of abortion, war, and care of the aged and dying. A consistent ethic of life encourages the specific concerns of each constituency, but also calls them to see the interrelatedness of their efforts. The need to defend the integrity of the moral principle in the full range of its application is a responsibility of each distinct constituency. If the principle is eroded in the public mind, all lose.

A second level of a consistent ethic stresses the distinction among cases rather than their similarities. We need different moral principles to apply to diverse cases. The classical distinction between ordinary and extraordinary means has applicability in the care of the dying but no relevance in the case of warfare. Not all moral principles have relevance across the whole range of life issues. Moreover, sometimes a systemic vision of the life issues requires a combination of moral insights to provide direction on one issue. . . . [In a previous speech] I cited the classical teaching on capital punishment which gives the state the right to take life in defense of key social values. But I also pointed out how a concern for promoting a *public attitude* of respect for life has led the bishops of the United States to oppose the *exercise* of that right.

. . . Abortion and capital punishment are not identical issues. The principle which protects *innocent* life distinguishes the unborn child from the convicted murderer. Other letters stress that while nuclear war is a threat to life, abortion involves the actual *taking* of a life, here and now. I accept both of these distinctions, of course, but I also find compelling the need to *relate* the cases while keeping them in distinct categories. Abortion is taking of life in ever-growing numbers in our society. Those concerned about it, I believe, will find their case enhanced by taking note of the rapidly expanding use of public execution. In a similar way, those who are particularly concerned about these executions, even if the accused has taken another life, should recognize the elementary truth that a society which can be indifferent to the innocent life of an unborn child will not be easily stirred to concern for a convicted criminal. There is, I maintain, a political and psychological linkage among the life issues—from war to welfare concerns—which we ignore at our own peril: a systemic vision of life seeks to expand the moral imagination of a society, not partition it into airtight categories.

A third level of the question before us involves how we relate a commitment to principles to our public witness of life. As I have said, no one can do everything. There are limits to both competency and energy; both point to the wisdom of setting priorities and defining distinct functions. The Church, however, must be credible across a wide range of issues; the very scope of our moral vision re-

The Nuclear Arms Race

In the 1980s, when Bernardin gave this speech, relations between the United States and the then Soviet Union were tense because of the race to stockpile nuclear weapons. These weapons continue to threaten world peace today, as nuclear programs spread in nations around the world, some of which are politically unstable.

quires a commitment to a multiplicity of questions. In this way the teaching of the Church will sustain a variety of individual commitments. . . .

A fourth level, one where dialogue is sorely needed, is the relationship between moral principles and concrete political choices. The moral questions of abortion, the arms race, the fate of social programs for the poor, and the role of human rights in foreign policy are *public* moral issues. The arena in which they are ultimately decided is not the academy or the Church but the political process. A consistent ethic of life seeks to present a coherent linkage among a diverse set of issues. It can and should be used to test party platforms, public policies, and political candidates. The Church legitimately fulfills a public role by articulating a framework for political choices, by relating that framework to specific issues, and by calling for systematic moral analysis of all areas of public policy. . . .

The Seamless Garment: A Pastoral and Public Contribution

The moral teaching of the Church has both pastoral and public significance. Pastorally, a consistent ethic of life is a contribution to the witness of the Church's defense of the human person. Publicly, a consistent ethic fills a void in our public policy debate today. . . .

The public value of a consistent ethic of life is connected directly to its pastoral role. In the public arena we should always speak and act like a Church. But the unique public possibility for a consistent ethic is provided precisely by the unstructured character of the public debate on the life questions. Each of the issues I have identified today—abortion, war, hunger and human rights, euthanasia, and capital punishment—is treated as a separate, self-contained topic in our public life. Each is distinct, but an ad hoc approach to each one fails to illustrate how our choices in one area can affect our decisions in other areas. There must be a public attitude of respect for all of life if public actions are to respect it in concrete cases.

. . . I am convinced there is an "open moment" before us on the agenda of life issues. It is a significant opportunity for the Church to demonstrate the strength of a sustained moral vision. I submit that a clear witness to a consistent ethic of life will allow us to grasp the opportunity of this "open moment" and serve both the sacredness of every human life and the God of Life who is the origin and support of our common humanity.

For Reflection

1. Based on the first part of the speech, "The Logic of the Case," what is our personal responsibility in cultivating a consistent ethic of life?

2. What does Bernardin identify as the four levels of a consistent ethic of life? Briefly summarize each in your own words.

3. What specific life issues does Bernardin address at the end of the excerpt? What does he mean when he says that "an ad hoc approach to each one fails"? Do you agree or disagree with this point? Explain your response.

4. What does Cardinal Bernardin mean when he says that "a systemic vision of life seeks to expand the moral imagination of a society"?

11 A Christian Vision of Marriage

Introduction

The year is 1953, and the third annual Emmy Awards ceremony is being broadcast from Los Angeles. The announcer calls out the category of "most outstanding television personality." The award goes to . . . Fulton J. Sheen, the host of *Life Is Worth Living*! Sheen walks to the microphone and proceeds to thank the four writers of his show: Matthew, Mark, Luke, and John.

Who was this outstanding television personality? Sheen was a Catholic bishop who brought the Gospel of Jesus and the teachings of the Church to an estimated weekly audience of 30 million viewers in the early days of television, after many years spent hosting a similar radio show. With charm, humor, and a keen intellect, he taught about a wide range of topics in a way that appealed to people of all ages and religions. Sheen became a respected, familiar, and beloved voice of the Catholic intellectual tradition. With a doctorate in philosophy, he infused his writing (more than sixty books), radio show (which ran for twenty years), and television show (which ran for fifteen years) with philosophical wisdom, wit, and morality. Even today, you can experience his timeless teachings through the syndication of his show and his published works.

Sheen's 1951 book *Three to Get Married* is a Christian vision of marriage that sees Jesus Christ at the heart of loving and chaste marriages. In the following reading from that book, Sheen contrasts sexual attraction with abiding marital love: "The greatest illusion of lovers is to believe that the intensity of their sexual attraction is the guarantee of the perpetuity of their love" (p. 1). Love has not only a physiological dimension—namely sexual attraction—but also psychological and spiritual dimensions, he explains.

We disregard these multiple dimensions of love at our peril. "There is no such thing as giving the body without giving the soul," writes Sheen of the human person (p. 2). Not merely sexual animals, we are also rational animals capable of communion with another through love, in all its human and divine expressions. Reminding us that we become what we love, in this excerpt Sheen maps out a loving and moral path for us to follow to relate to ourselves, to others, and to the Divine in a holy way.

Excerpt from *Three to Get Married*

By Archbishop Fulton J. Sheen

It takes three to make Love in Heaven—
Father, Son, and Holy Spirit. . . .

It takes three to make love in hearts—
The Lover, the Beloved, and Love.

I. The Differences between Sex and Love

Love is primarily in the will, not in the emotions or the glands. The will is like the voice; the emotions are like the echo. The *pleasure* associated with love, or what is today called "sex," is the frosting on the cake; its purpose is to make us love the cake, not ignore it. The greatest illusion of lovers is to believe that the intensity of their sexual attraction is the guarantee of the perpetuity of their love. It is because of this failure to distinguish between the glandular and spiritual—or between sex, which we have in common with animals, and love, which we have in common with God—that marriages are so full of deception. What some people love is not a person but the experience of being in love. The first is irreplaceable; the second is not. As soon as the glands cease to react with their pristine force, couples who identified emotionalism and love claim they no longer love one another. If such is the case, they never loved the other person in the first place; they only loved being loved, which is the highest form of egotism. Marriage founded on sex passion alone lasts only as long as the animal passion lasts. Within two years the animal attraction for the other may

> **carnal license** Permission or freedom to act in a way that promotes earthly, bodily, or sexual pleasure.

die, and when it does, law comes to its rescue to justify the divorce with the meaningless words "incompatibility" or "mental torture." Animals never have recourse to law courts, because they have no will to love; but man, having reason, feels the need of justifying his irrational behavior when he does wrong.

There are two reasons for the primacy of sex over love in a decadent civilization. One is the decline of reason. As humans give up reason, they resort to their imaginations. That is why movies and picture magazines enjoy such popularity. As thinking fades, unrestrained desires come to the fore. Since physical and erotic desires are among the easiest to dwell upon, because they require no effort and because they are powerfully aided by bodily passions, sex begins to be all-important. It is by no historical accident that an age of anti-intellectualism and irrationalism, such as our own, is also an age of **carnal license**.

The second factor is egotism. As belief in a Divine Judgment, a future life, heaven and hell, a moral order, is increasingly rejected, the ego becomes more and more firmly enthroned as the source of its morality. Each person becomes a judge in his own case. With this increase of selfishness, the demands for self-satisfaction become more and more imperious, and the interests of the community and the rights of others have less and less appeal. All sin is self-centeredness, as love is otherness and relatedness. Sin is the infidelity of man to the image of what he ought to be in his eternal vocation as an adopted son of God: the image God sees in Himself when He contemplates His Word.

There are two extremes to be avoided in discussing married love: one is the refusal to recognize sexual love, the other is the giving of primacy to sexual attraction. The first error was Victorian; the second is Freudian. To the Christian, sex is inseparable from the person, and to reduce the person to sex is as silly as to reduce personality to lungs or a thorax. Certain Victorians in their education practically denied sex as a function

Victorian and Freudian Views of Sexuality

In nineteenth-century Victorian society, people's understanding of sexuality commonly included repressive norms that did not adequately reflect the totality of the human person. In contrast, the Freudian view of sexuality developed in the late nineteenth and early twentieth century through the work of Sigmund Freud, who viewed the human person as a creature driven by sexual appetite.

of personality; certain sexophiles of modern times deny personality and make a god of sex. The male animal is attracted to the female animal, but a human personality is attracted to another human personality. The attraction of beast to beast is physiological; the attraction of human to human is physiological, psychological, and spiritual. The human spirit has a thirst for the infinite that the **quadruped** has not. This infinite is really God. But man can pervert that thirst, which the animal cannot because it has no concept of the infinite. Infidelity in married life is basically the substitution for an infinite of a succession of finite carnal experiences. The false infinity of succession takes the place of the Infinity of Destiny, which is God. The beast is promiscuous for an entirely different reason than man. The false pleasure given by new conquests in the realm of sex is the **ersatz** for the conquest of the Spirit in the Sacrament! The sense of emptiness, melancholy, and frustration is a consequence of the failure to find infinite satisfaction in what is carnal and limited. Despair is disappointed **hedonism**. The most depressed spirits are those who seek God in a false god!

If love does not climb, it falls. If, like the flame, it does not burn upward to the sun, it burns downward to destroy. If sex does not mount to heaven, it descends into hell. There is no such thing as giving the body without giving the soul. Those who think they can be faithful in soul to one another, but unfaithful in body, forget that the two are inseparable. Sex in isolation from personality does not exist! An arm living and gesticulating apart from the living organism is an impossibility. Man has no organic functions isolated from his soul. There is involvement of the whole personality. Nothing is more **psychosomatic** than the union of two in one flesh; nothing so much alters a mind, a will, for better or for worse. The separation of soul and body is death. Those who separate sex and spirit are rehearsing for death. The enjoyment of the other's personality through one's own personality is love. The pleasure of animal function through another's animal function is sex separated from love.

Sex is one of the means God has instituted for the enrichment of personality. It is a basic principle of philosophy that there is nothing in the mind that was not previously in the senses. All our knowledge comes from the body. We have a body, St. Thomas [Aquinas] tells us, because of the weakness of our intellect. Just as the enrichment of the mind comes from the body and its senses, so the enrichment of love comes through the body and its sex. As one can see a universe mirrored in a tear on a cheek, so in sex can be seen mirrored that wider world of love. Love in monogamous marriage includes sex; but sex, in the contemporary use of the term, does not imply either marriage or monogamy. . . .

But when sex is divorced from love there is a feeling that one has been stopped at the vestibule of the castle of pleasure; that the heart has been denied the city after crossing the bridge. Sadness and melancholy result from such a frustration of destiny, for it is the nature of man to be sad when he is pulled outside himself, or exteriorized, without getting any nearer his goal. There is a closer correlation between mental instability and the animal view of sex than many suspect. Happiness consists in interiority of the spirit, namely, the development of personality in relationship to a heavenly destiny. He who has no purpose in life is unhappy; he who exteriorizes his life and is dominated, or subjugated, by what is outside himself, or spends his energy on the external without understanding its mystery, is unhappy to the point of melancholy. There is the feeling of being hungry after having eaten or of being disgusted with food, because it has nourished not the body, in the case of an individual, or another body, in the case of marriage. . . . Two glasses that

quadruped A four-legged animal.

ersatz An artificial, often inferior substitute for something genuine.

hedonism Attitude that values the seeking of worldly pleasure, especially sensual pleasure.

psychosomatic Relating to both the mind and the body.

are empty cannot fill up one another. There must be a fountain of water outside the glasses, in order that they may have communion with one another. It takes three to make love.

Every person is what he loves. Love becomes like unto that which it loves. If it loves heaven, it becomes heavenly; if it loves the carnal as a god, it becomes corruptible. The kind of immortality we have depends on the kind of loves we have. Putting it negatively, he who tells you what he does not love, also tells what he is. "*Amor pondus meum*: Love is my gravitation," said St. Augustine. This slow conversion of a subject into an object, of a lover into the beloved, of the miser into his gold, of the saint into his God, discloses the importance of loving the right things. The nobler our loves, the nobler our character. To love what is below the human is degradation; to love what is human for the sake of the human is mediocrity; to love the human for the sake of the Divine is enriching; to love the Divine for its own sake is sanctity.

> 66 *Every person is what he loves. Love becomes like unto that which it loves.* 99

For Reflection

1. According to Sheen, what two factors promote "sex over love in a decadent civilization"? Summarize each in your own words. Do you agree or disagree with his reasons, and why?

2. Sheen says that infidelity substitutes "an infinite" with "a succession of finite carnal experiences." What do you think he means?

3. Why does Sheen teach that one cannot give the body without also "giving the soul"? How do you respond to this point?

4. Explain Sheen's analogy of the two empty glasses. How does the final paragraph of this excerpt relate to his empty glass analogy?

12 The Little Way of Living the Great Commandments

Introduction

"I want to be a warrior, a priest, an apostle, a Doctor of the Church, a martyr . . . I would like to perform the most heroic deeds," wrote Saint Thérèse of Lisieux (1873–1897) in her spiritual autobiography. But her bold passion contrasted with her humility, or what she called the "littleness" of her life.

At fifteen years of age, Thérèse Martin entered a **cloistered** Carmelite order of nuns in Lisieux, France. At age twenty-four she died of tuberculosis, having never again left the convent's walls. Few people knew this young nun in her lifetime. But through the publication of her autobiography after her death, Thérèse, often called the Little Flower of Jesus, became known worldwide. *The Story of a Soul* eventually was translated into fifty languages. Thérèse is one of the best-known, well-loved saints of the twentieth century. What draws people to Thérèse and her story? Her simple spirituality, her "little way" to Heaven.

This chapter's reading, from *The Story of a Soul,* introduces Thérèse's little way to heaven. Although most of us, like Thérèse, cannot claim to have committed great acts of heroism, she explains how each of our lives can be a testimony built of small acts of kindness and love that make the world a better place. Holiness is attainable through Thérèse's little way of love.

In this selection Thérèse examines the virtue of charity, one kind of love. Today we might think of charity as an act of goodwill, often in the form of donating money or time. But

> **cloistered** Adjective indicating a religious order whose members rarely leave the monastery or convent that is their home.

charity is so much more. Through charity, one of the **theological virtues**, we love God above all things and, out of that love of God, love our neighbors as ourselves. In the Gospel of Matthew, Jesus summarizes the laws of the Old Testament with these two laws of love, the Two Great Commandments: "You shall love the Lord, your God, with all your heart, with all your soul, and with all your mind. This is the greatest and the first commandment. The second is like it: You shall love your neighbor as yourself" (22:37–39). It is this love, the expression of true charity toward God and neighbor, that Thérèse of Lisieux examines in this reading from *The Story of a Soul*.

Thérèse says that when she became aware that her charity toward others was imperfect, she sought to correct this by practicing little acts of kindness through the grace of God. She tried to love as Jesus would love—expressing this love not merely in feelings but also in actions. Like all of us, Thérèse liked some people and found others irritating. But she worked hard to extend charity to all she encountered. "We naturally like to please a friend, but that is not charity, for so do sinners," she explains. True charity means showing love and kindness to all of our neighbors.

So Thérèse says she began to focus on the virtuous characteristics in others, not on their faults and failures, and she praised God for their positive qualities. In little ways she sought to channel God's love for her neighbor. This simple "little way" spirituality of Saint Thérèse of Lisieux was one factor that earned her the title Doctor of the Church.

Thérèse addresses her writing to "Mother," the Mother Superior of her convent, who directed Thérèse to write her autobiography. But through her story, Thérèse calls all of us to follow her little lessons about true charity, the love of God and neighbor. We too can "aim at being a saint" by following her little way to Heaven.

Excerpt from *The Story of a Soul*
By Saint Thérèse of Lisieux

How different, Lord, are the paths along which You guide souls! In the lives of the saints we find many who left nothing behind them, not the smallest souvenir or a scrap of writing. But there are others, like our Mother St. Teresa, who have enriched the Church by their teaching. They were not afraid to reveal "the secrets of the King," so that souls, by knowing Him better, would love Him more. Which kind of life is most pleasing to Our Lord? I think both are equally acceptable. All those loved by God have followed the prompting of the Holy Ghost, who made the prophet write: "Tell the just man that all is well." Yes, all is well when one tries to do nothing but God's will. . . .

You know, Mother, that I have always wanted to become a saint. Unfortunately when I have compared myself with the saints, I have always found that there is the same difference between the saints and me as there is between a mountain whose summit is lost in the clouds and a humble grain of sand trodden underfoot by passersby. Instead of being discouraged, I told myself: God would not make me wish for

Saint Teresa of Ávila and the Carmelites

The Carmelites are a contemplative religious order founded in the twelfth century. Mother St. Teresa, to whom Saint Thérèse refers, is the great sixteenth-century reformer of the Carmelite order, Saint Teresa of Ávila.

something impossible and so, in spite of my littleness, I can aim at being a saint. It is impossible for me to grow bigger, so I put up with myself as I am, with all my countless faults. But I will look for some means of going to heaven by a little way which is very short and very straight, a little way that is quite new. We live in an age of inventions. We need no longer climb laboriously up flights of stairs; in well-to-do houses there are **lifts**. And I was determined to find a lift to carry me to Jesus, for I was far too small to climb the steep stairs of perfection. So I sought in Holy Scripture some idea of what this lift I wanted would be, and I read these words from the very mouth of eternal Wisdom: "Whosoever is a little one, let him come to me." I drew nearer to God, fully realising that I had found what I was looking for. I also wanted to know how God would deal with a "little one," so I continued my search and found this: "You shall be carried at the breasts and upon the knees; as one whom the mother caresseth, so will I comfort you." Never before had I been gladdened by such sweet and tender words. It is Your arms, Jesus, which are the lift to carry me to heaven. . . .

Among the countless graces I have received this year, perhaps the greatest has been that of being able to grasp in all its fulness the meaning of charity. I had never before fathomed Our Lord's words: "The second commandment is like to the first: Thou shalt love thy neighbour as thyself." I had striven above all to love God, and in loving Him I discovered the secret of those other words: "Not everyone that saith to me: Lord, Lord! shall enter into the **kingdom of heaven**, but he that doeth the will of my Father." Jesus made me understand what this will was by the words He used at the Last Supper when He gave His "new commandment" and told His apostles "to love one another as He had loved them." I began to consider just how Jesus had loved His disciples. I saw it was not for their natural

lifts Elevators.

Kingdom of Heaven The culmination or goal of God's plan of salvation, the Kingdom of Heaven, or Kingdom of God, is announced by the Gospel and present in Jesus Christ. The Kingdom is the reign or rule of God over the hearts of people and, as a consequence of that, the development of a new social order based on unconditional love.

qualities, for I recognised they were ignorant men and often preoccupied with earthly affairs. Yet He calls them His friends and His brethren. He wants to see them near Him in the kingdom of His Father and to open this kingdom to them. He wills to die on the Cross, saying: "Greater love than this no man hath, that a man lay down his life for his friends." As I meditated

> ❝ *I will look for some means of going to heaven by a little way which is very short and very straight, a little way that is quite new.* ❞

on these words of Jesus, I saw how imperfect was my love for the other nuns and I knew that I did not love them as Jesus loves them. But now I realise that true charity consists in putting up with all one's neighbour's faults, never being surprised by his weakness, and being inspired by the least of his virtues. Above all, I learnt that charity is not something that stays shut up in one's heart for "no man lighteth a candle and putteth it in a hidden place, nor under a bushel; but upon a candle-stick, that they who come in may see the light." This candle represents that charity which must illumine and cheer not only those dearest to me but "All those who are of the household."

When God, under the old law, told His people to love their neighbours as themselves, He had not yet come down to earth. As He knew how much we love ourselves, He could not ask us to do more. But when Jesus gave His apostles a "new commandment, His own commandment," He did not ask only that we should love our neighbours as ourselves but that we should love them as He loves them and as He will love them to the end of time. O Jesus, I know You command nothing that is impossible. You know how weak and imperfect I am, and You know only too well that I could never love the other nuns as You love them if You Yourself did not love them *within me*. It is because You wish to grant me this grace that You have given a new commandment. How I cherish it, for it assures me that it is Your will *to love in me* all those whom You command me to love.

When I act and think with charity, I feel it is Jesus who works within me. The closer I am united with Him, the more I love all the other dwellers in Carmel [the convent]. If I want this love to grow deeper and the devil tries to show me the faults of a sister, I hasten to think of all her virtues and of how good her intentions are. I tell myself that though I have seen her commit a sin, she may very well have won many spiritual victories of which I know nothing because of her humility. What seems a fault to me may very well be an act of virtue because of the intention behind it. . . .

To return to the Gospels where Our Lord teaches me so clearly what His new commandment is. In St. Matthew I read: "You have heard that it hath been said, Thou shall love thy neighbour and hate thy enemy: but I say unto you, love your enemies and pray for them that persecute you." In Carmel, of course, one has no enemies, but one certainly has natural likes and dislikes. One feels attracted to a certain sister and one would go out of one's way to dodge meeting another. Jesus tells me that it is this very sister I must love, and I must pray for her even though her attitude makes me believe she has no love for me. "If you love them that love you, what thanks are to you? For sinners also love those that love them." It is not enough to love. We must prove that we do. We naturally like to please a friend, but that is not charity, for so do sinners.

Jesus also teaches me: "Give to everyone that asketh thee; and of him that taketh away thy goods, ask them not again." It is not so pleasant to give to everyone who asks as it is to offer something freely and spontaneously; and it is easy to give when you are asked nicely, but if we are asked tactlessly, we at once want to refuse unless perfect charity strengthens us. We find a thousand reasons for saying no, and it is not until we have made the sister aware of her bad manners that we give her what she wants *as a favour,* or do her a slight service which takes a quarter of the time needed to tell her of the obstacles preventing our doing it or of our fancied rights. . . .

Oh, how contrary to human nature are the divine teachings! Without the help of grace, it would be impossible not only to follow them but even to understand them. . . .

Formerly one of our nuns managed to irritate me whatever she did or said. The devil was mixed up in it, for it was certainly he who made me see so many disagreeable traits in her. As I did not want to give way to my natural dislike for her, I told myself that charity should not only be a matter of feeling but should show itself in deeds. So I set myself to do for this sister just what I should have done for someone I loved most dearly. Every time I met her, I prayed for her and offered God all her virtues and her merits. I was sure this would greatly delight Jesus, for every artist likes to have his works praised

The Imitation Refers to *The Imitation of Christ*, a guide to moral living written by Thomas à Kempis in the fifteenth century.

and the divine Artist of souls is pleased when we do not halt outside the exterior of the sanctuary where He has chosen to dwell but go inside and admire its beauty.

I did not remain content with praying a lot for this nun who caused me so much disturbance. I tried to do as many things for her as I could, and whenever I was tempted to speak unpleasantly to her, I made myself give her a pleasant smile and tried to change the subject. *The Imitation* says: "It is more profitable to leave to everyone his way of thinking than to give way to contentious discourses."

. . . And after all this she asked me one day with a beaming face: "Sister Thérèse, will you please tell me what attracts you so much to me? You give me such a charming smile whenever we meet." Ah! it was Jesus hidden in the depth of her soul who attracted me, Jesus who makes the bitterest things sweet!

For Reflection

1. What lift, or elevator, does Thérèse say she found to carry her to Heaven? Explain in your own words.

2. Based upon what Thérèse says in this reading, what does charity require, and why? Create your own list of ways you can demonstrate true charity.

3. Thérèse writes about a nun whom she disliked. How did she balance her negative feelings? According to Thérèse, why would that have been pleasing to Jesus? How did the nun respond to her actions?

13 Living Life for Others

Introduction

An American B-29 bomber could be heard flying over the city of Hiroshima, Japan, on August 6, 1945. The warning sirens wailed, and then there was a blast like no other.

Fr. Pedro Arrupe, SJ, master of novices at a Jesuit seminary on the outskirts of Hiroshima, immediately transformed his novitiate into a makeshift hospital to care for some of the hundreds of thousands of casualties from that first atomic bomb. A medical student in his native Spain before he entered the Society of Jesus, Arrupe attended to the overflowing wounded. The world was forever changed by that atomic bomb, and so was Arrupe. Having personally encountered the horrors of war, he envisioned and actively worked toward a moral world of peace and justice, a world in which we live for one another.

In the 1960s Arrupe became superior general, or head, of the Society of Jesus, serving in this capacity for almost twenty years. From this position of leadership, he prompted his fellow Jesuits to be a voice for the voiceless, to educate for justice, to work in solidarity with those who suffer, and to be people of service for others. An **apostolate** of the Jesuit Order is education; well-known Jesuit universities in the United States include Georgetown, Fordham, Creighton, and Loyola. The first reading of this chapter comes from a 1973 speech that Arrupe delivered to the alumni of Jesuit schools throughout the world on July 31, the feast of Saint Ignatius of Loyola, the

apostolate The Christian person's (or community's) activity that fulfills the apostolic nature of the whole Church when he or she works to extend the Kingdom of Christ to the entire world.

founder of the Jesuits. Arrupe issued a challenge to these educated men and women, calling them to confront the injustices of the world and to live their lives out of love for others.

Although his speech was directed to Jesuit alumni, Arrupe's challenge is fitting for all of us. He admonishes us to go outside ourselves in love and service, rather than making ourselves the center of our own worlds. By cultivating an attitude of love and service, we not only humanize the world but also realize our own human potential. Arrupe urges us to break free from selfish thoughts and behaviors that lead to a downward spiral of ambition, competition, and self-destruction. Instead he calls us to adjust our actions and attitudes so that we may live more simply and be agents of change in society—in essence, to be men and women for others.

The second reading here could be considered a poem in prose. Although its origin is unknown, some attribute it to a spontaneous speech made by Arrupe. Certainly, it is consistent with Arrupe's message in the first reading, but it expands the message with one important reminder: It is God's love that enables and empowers us to live life for others.

Excerpt from "Men and Women for Others"
By Pedro Arrupe, SJ

The Men and Women the Church Needs Today. What kind of man or woman is needed today by the church, by the world? One who is a "man-for-others," a "woman-for-others." That is my shorthand description. A man-or-woman-for-others. But does this not contradict the very nature of the human person? Are we not each a "being-for-ourselves"? Gifted with intelligence that endows us with power, do we not tend to control the world, making ourselves its center? Is this not our vocation, our history?

Yes. Gifted with conscience, intelligence, and power each of us is indeed a center. But a center called to go out of ourselves, to give ourselves to others in love—love, which is our definitive and all-embracing dimension, that which gives meaning to all our other dimensions. Only those who love fully realize themselves as persons. To the extent that any of us shut ourselves off from others we do not become more a person; we become less.

Those who live only for their own interests not only provide nothing for others. They do worse. They tend to accumulate in exclusive fashion more and more knowledge, more and more power, more and more wealth; thus denying, inevitably to those weaker than themselves their proper share of the God-given means for human development.

What is it to humanize the world if not to put it at the service of humankind? But egoists not only do not humanize the material creation; they **dehumanize** others. They change others into things by dominating them, exploiting them, and taking to themselves the fruit of their labor.

The tragedy of it all is that by doing this, egoists dehumanize themselves. They surrender themselves to the possessions they covet. They become their slave—no longer persons who are self-possessed but un-persons, things driven by their blind desires and their objects.

But when we dehumanize, depersonalize ourselves in this way, something stirs within us. We feel frustrated. In our heart of hearts we know that what we have is nothing compared with what we are, what we can be, what we would like to be. We would like to be ourselves. But we dare not break the vicious circle. We think we can overcome our frustrations by striving to have more, to have more than others, to have ever more and more. We thus turn our lives into a competitive rat-race without meaning.

The downward spiral of ambition, competition, and self-destruction twists and expands unceasingly, with the result that we are chained ever more securely to a progressive, and progressively frustrating, dehumanization.

Dehumanization of ourselves and dehumanization of others. For by thus making egoism a way of life, we translate it, we objectify it, in social structures. Starting from our individual sins of egoism, we become exploiters of others, dehumanizing them and ourselves in the process,

dehumanize To act in ways that degrade or deny the innate dignity of the human person; to deprive someone of basic human rights.

and hardening the process into a structure of society which may rightfully be called sin objectified. For it becomes hardened in ideas, institutions, impersonal and depersonalized organisms which now escape our direct control, a tyrannical power of destruction and self-destruction.

How escape from this vicious circle? Clearly, the whole process has its root in egoism—in the denial of love. But to try to live in love and justice in a world whose prevailing climate is egoism and injustice, where egoism and injustice are built into the very structures of society—is this not a suicidal, or at least a fruitless undertaking?

And yet, it lies at the very core of the Christian message. It is the sum and substance of the call of Christ. St. Paul put it in a single sentence: "Do not allow yourself to be overcome by evil, but rather, overcome evil with good" (Rom. 12:21). This teaching, which is identical with the teaching of Christ about love for the enemy, is the touchstone of Christianity. All of us would like to be good to others, and most of us would be relatively good in a good world. What is difficult is to be good in an evil world, where the egoism of others and the egoism built into the institutions of society attack us and threaten to annihilate us.

Under such conditions, the only possible reaction would seem to be to oppose evil with evil, egoism with egoism, hate with hate; in short, to annihilate the aggressor with his own weapons. But is it not precisely thus that evil conquers us most thoroughly? For then, not only does it damage us exteriorly, it perverts our very heart. We allow ourselves, in the words of St. Paul, to be overcome by evil.

No. Evil is overcome only by good, hate by love, egoism by generosity. It is thus that we must sow justice in our world. To be just, it is not enough to refrain from injustice. One must go further and refuse to play its game, substituting love for self-interest as the driving force of society.

All this sounds very nice, you will say, but isn't it just a little bit up in the air? Very well, let us get down to cases. How do we get this principle of justice through love down to the level of reality, the reality of our daily lives? By cultivating in ourselves three attitudes:

First, a firm determination to live much more simply—as individuals, as families, as social groups—and in this way to stop short, or at least to slow down, the expanding spiral of luxurious living and social competi-

> **Consumer Society**
>
> A consumer society is built on an economic system that encourages the buying and selling of merchandise with little regard for the long-range social, financial, or environmental implications of this consumption. In a consumer society, consumption and the acquisition of material possessions are principal aspirations.

tion. Let us have men and women who will resolutely set themselves against the tide of our consumer society. Men and women who, instead of feeling compelled to acquire everything that their friends have will do away with many of the luxuries which in their social set have become necessities, but which the majority of humankind must do without. And if this produces surplus income, well and good; let it be given to those for whom the necessities of life are still luxuries beyond their reach.

Second, a firm determination to draw no profit whatever from clearly unjust sources. Not only that, but going further, to diminish progressively our share in the benefits of an economic and social system in which the rewards of production accrue to those already rich, while the cost of production lies heavily on the poor. Let there be men and women who will bend their energies not to strengthen positions of privilege, but to the extent possible reduce privilege in favor of the underprivileged. Please do not conclude too hastily that this does not pertain to you, that you do not belong to the privileged few in your society. It touches everyone of a certain social position, even though only in certain respects, and even if we ourselves may be the victims of unjust discrimination by those who are even better off than ourselves. In this matter, our basic point of reference must be the truly poor, the truly marginalized, in our own countries and in the Third World.

Third and most difficult: a firm resolve to be agents of change in society not merely resisting unjust structures and arrangements, but actively undertaking to reform them. For, if we set out to reduce income insofar as it is derived from participation in unjust structures, we will find out soon enough that we are faced with an impossible task unless those very structures are changed.

Thus, stepping down from our own posts of power would be too simple a course of action. In certain circumstances it may be the proper thing to do; but ordinarily it merely serves to hand over the entire social structure to the exploitation of the egotistical. Here precisely is where we begin to feel how difficult is the struggle for justice. . . .

. . . For in the last analysis, it is the oppressed who must be the principal agents of change. The role of the privileged is to assist them, to reinforce with pressure from above the pressure exerted from below on the structures that need to be changed.

Men-and-women-for-others: the paramount objective of Jesuit education—basic, advanced, and continuing—must now be to form such men and women. For if there is any substance in our reflections, then this is the prolongation into the modern world of our humanist tradition as derived from the Spiritual Exercises of St. Ignatius. Only by being a man-or-woman-for-others does one become fully human, not only in the merely natural sense, but in the sense of being the "spiritual" person of St. Paul. The person filled with the Spirit; and we know whose

> " *Only by being a man-or-woman-for-others does one become fully human.* "

Spirit that is: the Spirit of Christ, who gave his life for the salvation of the world; the God who, by becoming a human person, became, beyond all others, a Man-for-others, a Woman-for-others.

"Love Will Decide Everything"
Attributed to Pedro Arrupe, SJ

Nothing is more practical than finding God, that is, than falling in love in a quite absolute, final way. What you are in love with, what seizes your imagination, will affect everything. It will decide what will get you out of bed in the morning, what you will do with your evenings, how you will spend your weekends, what you read, who you know, what breaks your heart, and what amazes you with joy and gratitude. Fall in love, stay in love, and it will decide everything.

For Reflection

1. Using the concepts Arrupe outlined in this reading, describe an "egoist" as he would define the term.

2. According to Arrupe, what teaching is the touchstone of Christianity? What makes it difficult to follow this teaching? How does he say that we can best live according to this touchstone?

3. What three attitudes does Arrupe advocate to guide the principle of justice, and why? Choose one of these attitudes, and give a concrete example of how you could live accordingly.

4. The second reading, "Love Will Decide Everything," says that what we love affects everything we do. What does this mean? Do you agree or disagree? Explain your response.

Part 3

Moral Lessons in Loving God and Neighbor

14 Grace and Spirit

Introduction

It is a blustery day. The wind dances with the trees; their branches sway to and fro as their leaves shimmy and shake. Can you actually see this wind? Perhaps not, but you can see its effects. **Grace** is like the wind.

God's abundant grace can be seen through those who strive to live a life in Christ. In the following excerpt from his book *Introducing Moral Theology: True Happiness and the Virtues,* William C. Mattison III uses the Christian wisdom of C. S. Lewis to explore how grace empowers us to live the Christian moral life. Mattison, a professor of moral theology at the Catholic University of America, specializes in **virtue** ethics, teaching on such basic questions as why we should be moral. *Introducing Moral Theology* is a textbook he wrote to address students' fundamental moral questions through the lens of virtue and the human quest for happiness. In the excerpt in this chapter, he looks at grace, the "source and sustenance" of Christian morality (p. 313).

Although we can see the effects of God's grace, by what means is grace at work in our lives and in the world? Mattison

grace The free and undeserved gift of God's loving and active presence in the universe and in our lives, empowering us to respond to his call and to live as his adopted sons and daughters. Grace restores our loving communion with the Holy Trinity, lost through sin.

virtue A habitual and firm disposition to do good.

Holy Spirit The Third Person of the Blessed Trinity, understood as the perfect love between God the Father and the Son, Jesus Christ, who inspires, guides, and sanctifies the life of believers.

reminds us that grace is a gift from God through the **Holy Spirit**, whom God sent forth upon the earth after Jesus' Resurrection and Ascension. This enduring Spirit guides us to do what our human abilities alone cannot accomplish.

Certainly, Jesus' life alone can inspire us to lead good lives. In fact, as Mattison acknowledges, history has given us many great teachers and practitioners of moral living from whom we can learn. But although their example can inspire us to be people of virtue, they cannot actively promote our ability to be virtuous. In contrast, through the workings of the Holy Spirit in the form of grace, Jesus Christ is present today, actively helping us to be virtuous and moral—to be friends of God and to love our neighbor. Scripture and the Sacraments, prayer and the people in our lives—all are ways in which we can encounter this grace, which Mattison calls "God's real agency on us" (p. 314).

In this excerpt, Mattison helps us see how life in Christ helps us to live beyond our natural abilities so we can dance with the wind of grace and be channels of God's Spirit in our world today.

Excerpt from *Introducing Moral Theology: True Happiness and the Virtues*

By William C. Mattison III

Defining and Describing Grace

Christians commonly claim that they live "in Christ," or that Christ lives in them (Gal. 2:20, Rom. 8:2). What does this mean? . . . Much has been said of what a person living in Christ does. Less has been said on how it is done. Explicit and important discussion of grace has been missing.

As [C. S.] Lewis says aptly, Christians do not "act on their own steam."[1] The Christian is "nourishing and protecting a life that he could never have acquired through his own efforts."[2] The source and sustenance of that life is Christ. It is tempting to think that living out Christian disci-

C. S. Lewis (1893–1963)

Clive Staples Lewis was a British literary scholar and novelist who is probably remembered best for his Chronicles of Narnia, a series of children's Christian allegorical stories in which a lion, Aslan, serves as the Christ figure. Along with his close friend J. R. R. Tolkien, author of *The Hobbit* and *The Lord of the Rings*, Lewis was a member of an Oxford University literary group. Lewis's memoir *Surprised by Joy* is the story of his return to the Christian faith after falling away during his adolescence.

pleship is acting in accordance with Christian beliefs, and in a manner that mimics how Jesus Christ lived on earth. This is certainly true. But Christians think something more happens as well.

> Put right out of your head the idea that these [claims about living in Christ] are only fancy ways of saying that Christians are to read what Christ said and try to carry it out—as a man may read what **Plato** or Marx said and try to carry it out. They mean something much more than that. They mean that a real Person, here and now, in the very room where you are saying your prayers, *is doing things to you.* It is not a question of a good man who died two thousand years ago. It is a living Man, still as much a man as you, and still as much God as He was when He created the world, *really coming and interfering with your very self,* killing the old natural self in you and replacing it with the kind of self He has. At first only for moments. Then for longer periods. Finally, if all goes well, turning you permanently into a different sort of thing: into a new little Christ, a being which, in its own small way, has the same kind of life as God; which shares in His power, joy, knowledge, and eternity.[3]

The difference between a great moral teacher (such as, say, Plato) and Christ should now be more completely understood. A great moral teacher does not actively help one in the present to live out what is taught,

Plato Greek philosopher of the fourth century BC who founded the Academy in Athens; student of Socrates and teacher of Aristotle.

whereas Christians believe Christ does exactly this. Jesus Christ is the definitive event in human history, not only in a backward-looking way because he cleaned the slate, but also in a forward-looking way in that he lives on, assisting real people to live in Christ.

Grace is the term for this help that God gives people to know and live a more truthful, holy, and virtuous life, directed ultimately toward union with God. The grace of God has always been associated with the Holy Spirit, as when Jesus encountered his disciples after the Resurrection, "breathed on them, and said to them, 'Receive the Holy Spirit'" (John 20:22). The association of grace and the Holy Spirit can be seen in the traditional prayer, "Come Holy Spirit, fill the hearts of your faithful and kindle in them the fire of your love. Lord, send forth your Spirit, and renew the face of the earth." It is also seen in the seven

> *Jesus is the definitive event in human history, not only in a backward-looking way because he cleaned the slate, but also in a forward-looking way in that he lives on, assisting real people to live in Christ.*

traditional "gifts of the Holy Spirit," which are God's grace in helping a person to be docile to the promptings of the Holy Spirit. These seven gifts, derived from Isaiah 1:1–2, are: wisdom, understanding, counsel, fortitude, knowledge, piety, and fear of the Lord. Grace can be difficult to specify, for many reasons. One such reason is that if the Christian claim is true—that God is the source of all that is—what is *not* grace? First of all, anything that is not a help to live more holy and truthful lives is not help from God. So any expressions of our sinfulness, for example, are not in themselves works of God's grace. Second, grace should not be equated simply with goodness. There are indeed many good things that are from God, such as our capacities of reason and will. These things may be crucial on our journey toward our supernatural destiny, or union with God. But the more precise meaning of grace used here is not only what is good or done by God in some sense, but rather what is done by God that directs us to supernatural happiness in union with God. Grace is God's help to do things that are not possible with natural human capacities alone, since they direct us toward our supernatural destiny. Therefore, living a life in Christ, a life of grace, is not simply a matter of being our better selves rather than our sinful selves, and following a rightly formed conscience. It is receiving help from beyond us to direct us toward the ultimate purpose of union with God. "God is the one who, for his good purpose, works in you both to desire and to work" (Phil. 2:13).

One of the primary Christian claims about grace is that God is truly an agent when people live in Christ. This help from God is received in countless ways. One of the more obvious is through other people. Think of all the ways we receive this assistance through others. None of us could have the faith we do without having heard about God from others. Our friends often sustain us in living holy lives. Reading the scriptures, inspired as it is by the Holy Spirit and yet enfleshed in human language written by human authors, is another source of grace. The sacraments are excellent examples of God's real assistance in transforming our lives to be more Christlike. In times of prayer, as Lewis says, God works on us. It is perhaps easier to see how God's assistance comes concretely through prayer, the scriptures, and sacraments, since these are churchy activities. But we should not neglect the importance of how God works on us through other avenues, be they more exalted moments of inspiration from natural beauty, or in the everyday ways that those around us support and encourage us in living holy lives. This is a main reason why friendship is such an essential part of the virtuous life in Christ.

It is easy for the skeptic to see things differently, of course. Why label all of these influences as God's real agency on us? Why not just call them "good influences"? In one sense this is of course correct. All of these occasions are good influences on our lives. But their origin is God and not simply those persons who act as instruments of God's grace in our lives. To use another analogy from Lewis:

> At first it is natural for a baby to take its mother's milk without knowing its mother. It is equally natural for us to see the man who helps us without seeing Christ behind him. But we must not remain babies. We must go on to recognize the real Giver.[4]

Why must there be a real giver behind these influences? If the central claims of the Christian story . . . are true, then the life and destiny to which we are called is beyond our human capacities. We could not understand it without help from beyond us, and we could not live in accordance with it without God's help. This life could not be known and lived on our own, understanding "our" not just in individual but also in **corporate** terms.

corporate Collective or communal, as part of a group.

In sum, God's grace is at work when we receive help from God to know and do particular things we could not know and do on our own, things that reveal to us and lead us toward our destiny of complete happiness in union with God. It must be acknowledged by Christians that though grace can be described in an intellectually sound manner, the best proof of its existence is not theological discourse, but the real lived experiences of people caught up in the life of God.

Endnotes

1. C. S. Lewis, *Mere Christianity,* 63.
2. Ibid.
3. Ibid., 190 (emphasis added).
4. Ibid., 190–91.

Grace and Christian Confidence

The Little Engine That Could is a classic children's tale that teaches the power of positive thinking through a little steam engine who is trying to get to the other side of a mountain. Repeating, "I think I can, I think I can," the little engine successfully chugs up and over the mountain. Descending, the engine says, "I thought I could, I thought I could." For Christians, the "steam" of grace and Spirit is what empowers us to climb the moral mountains of our lives, saying assuredly, "I know I can, I know I can."

For Reflection

1. What does Mattison say is the difference between any moral teacher and Christ?

2. Mattison says, "One of the primary Christian claims about grace is that God is truly an agent when people live in Christ." What does it mean to say that God is an agent?

3. The reading states, "The life and destiny to which we are called is beyond our human capacities." According to Mattison and Lewis, why is that so? What helps us to respond to this call?

4. Although theology can try to explain the concept of grace, what is the greatest proof that grace exists, according to Mattison? Provide an example of this proof from your own experience.

15 What Would Jesus Do?

Introduction

Do you have someone in your life to whom you can always turn for really solid advice? Thomas à Kempis has provided sound moral guidance to hundreds of thousands of people for the last six hundred years.

Thomas à Kempis (1380–1471) was a German priest who lived in a monastic community. For a minute let us tune in to a conversation that might have happened within the monastery walls. Brother Monk says to Father Thomas, "I've been told that I act impulsively, and I really want to act more like Jesus. How can I be more like Christ?" Father Thomas kindly responds, "Do not yield to every impulse and suggestion but consider things carefully and patiently in the light of God's will." He goes on to explain the idea of prudence for this impulsive brother monk. The monk puts the advice into practice and discovers the wisdom of Thomas's guidance. He later encourages Thomas to put his ideas in writing for the other monks.

Thomas did write down his advice. The reading in this chapter comes from his book *The Imitation of Christ*, containing his words of wisdom for walking the Christian moral path. In Christian literature, it is the most widely translated book, second only to the Bible.

The reminder "What would Jesus do?" (WWJD) became popular among Christians in the United States in the 1990s. *The Imitation of Christ* is a fifteenth-century response to that modern question. But the idea of imitating Christ as we make moral choices goes back even further—it is found in the Good News proclaimed by Jesus and in his call to live as his disciples. Jesus says, "Whoever follows me will not walk in darkness, but will have the light of life" (John 8:12). Thomas places this call at the heart of his book from the very beginning: "By these words of

humility Derived from the Latin *humus*, meaning earth or ground. A Christian virtue and disposition that counters the vice of false pride; sometimes called the "queen of virtues," this attitude was modeled by Mary of Nazareth.

envy One of the seven deadly, or capital, sins; not merely wanting what another has (jealousy), but rather resenting the good fortune of another, which can lead to other deadly sins. This vice can be countered by the virtue of charity.

Christ we are advised to imitate His life and habits, if we wish to be truly enlightened and free from all blindness of heart. Let our chief effort, therefore, be to study the life of Jesus Christ" (book 1, chapter 1).

In the excerpts you will read here, Thomas gives practical and detailed advice on how to be more like Christ by cultivating **humility** and prudence to help us avoid the sins of pride and **envy**. You may even recognize some of the sayings in the reading, such as Thomas's observation that "an old habit is hard to break" (book 1, chapter 14). Many great saints over the centuries, including Thomas More, Ignatius of Loyola, and Thérèse of Lisieux, consulted this bestseller for moral guidance. When you read the selections here and seek to follow their wisdom, you will join centuries of holy men and women who have turned to Thomas à Kempis for help with living a good life in imitation of Christ.

Excerpts from *The Imitation of Christ*

By Thomas à Kempis

Book One: Thoughts Helpful in the Life of the Soul

The First Chapter: Imitating Christ and Despising All Vanities on Earth

"He who follows Me, walks not in darkness," says the Lord (John 8:12). By these words of Christ we are advised to imitate His life and habits, if we wish to be truly enlightened and free from all blindness of heart. Let our chief effort, therefore, be to study the life of Jesus Christ. . . .

The Fourth Chapter: Prudence in Action

Do not yield to every impulse and suggestion but consider things carefully and patiently in the light of God's will. For very often, sad to say, we are so weak that we believe and speak evil of others rather than good. Perfect men, however, do not readily believe every talebearer, because they know that human frailty is prone to evil and is likely to appear in speech.

Not to act rashly or to cling obstinately to one's opinion, not to believe everything people say or to spread abroad the gossip one has heard, is great wisdom.

Take counsel with a wise and conscientious man. Seek the advice of your betters in preference to following your own inclinations.

A good life makes a man wise according to God and gives him experience in many things, for the more humble he is and the more subject to God, the wiser and the more at peace he will be in all things.

> **Virtue and Vice**
>
> Thomas à Kempis uses the language of virtue and vice in *The Imitation of Christ*. Virtue is a habitual and firm disposition to do good, sometimes called moral excellence. The opposite of virtue is vice, a practice or habit that leads a person to sin. The three theological virtues (faith, hope, and love) and the four cardinal virtues (prudence, justice, temperance, and fortitude) stand in contrast to the vices that are sometimes called the seven deadly or capital sins: pride, wrath, greed, sloth, lust, envy, and gluttony.

The Seventh Chapter: Avoiding False Hope and Pride

Vain is the man who puts his trust in men, in created things.

Do not be ashamed to serve others for the love of Jesus Christ and to seem poor in this world. Do not be self-sufficient but place your trust in God. Do what lies in your power and God will aid your good will. Put no trust in your own learning nor in the cunning of any man, but rather in the grace of God Who helps the humble and humbles the proud.

If you have wealth, do not glory in it, nor in friends because they are powerful, but in God Who gives all things and Who desires above all to give Himself. Do not boast of personal stature or of physical beauty, qualities which are marred and destroyed by a little sickness. Do not take pride in your talent or ability, lest you displease God to Whom belongs all the natural gifts that you have.

Do not think yourself better than others lest, perhaps, you be accounted worse before God Who knows what is in man. Do not take pride in your good deeds, for God's judgments differ from those of men and what pleases them often displeases Him. If there is good in you, see more good in others, so that you may remain humble. It does no harm to esteem yourself less than anyone else, but it is very harmful to think yourself better than even one. The humble live in continuous peace, while in the hearts of the proud are envy and frequent anger.

The Fourteenth Chapter: Avoiding Rash Judgment

Turn your attention upon yourself and beware of judging the deeds of other men, for in judging others a man labors vainly, often makes mistakes, and easily sins; whereas, in judging and taking stock of himself he does something that is always profitable.

We frequently judge that things are as we wish them to be, for through personal feeling true perspective is easily lost.

If God were the sole object of our desire, we should not be disturbed so easily by opposition to our opinions. But often something lurks within or happens from without to draw us along with it.

Many, unawares, seek themselves in the things they do. They seem even to enjoy peace of mind when things happen according to their wish and liking, but if otherwise than they desire, they are soon disturbed and saddened. Differences of feeling and opinion often divide friends and acquaintances, even those who are religious and devout.

> **If God were the sole object of our desire, we should not be disturbed so easily by opposition to our opinions.**

An old habit is hard to break, and no one is willing to be led farther than he can see.

If you rely more upon your intelligence or industry than upon the virtue of submission to Jesus Christ, you will hardly, and in any case slowly, become an enlightened man. God wants us to be completely subject to Him and, through ardent love, to rise above all human wisdom.

Book Two: The Interior Life

The Second Chapter: Humility

Be not troubled about those who are with you or against you, but take care that God be with you in everything you do. Keep your conscience clear and God will protect you, for the malice of man cannot harm one whom God wishes to help. If you know how to suffer in silence, you will undoubtedly experience God's help. He knows when and how to deliver you; therefore, place yourself in His hands, for it is a divine prerogative to help men and free them from all distress.

It is often good for us to have others know our faults and rebuke them, for it gives us greater humility. When a man humbles himself because of his faults, he easily placates those about him and readily appeases those who are angry with him.

It is the humble man whom God protects and liberates; it is the humble whom He loves and consoles. To the humble He turns and upon them bestows great grace, that after their humiliation He may raise them up to glory. He reveals His secrets to the humble, and with kind invitation bids them come to Him. Thus, the humble man enjoys peace in the midst of many vexations, because his trust is in God, not in the world. Hence, you must not think that you have made any progress until you look upon yourself as inferior to all others.

The Fourth Chapter: Purity of Mind and Unity of Purpose

A man is raised up from the earth by two wings—simplicity and purity. There must be simplicity in his intention and purity in his desires. Simplicity leads to God, purity embraces and enjoys Him.

If your heart is free from ill-ordered affection, no good deed will be difficult for you. If you aim at and seek after nothing but the pleasure of God and the welfare of your neighbor, you will enjoy freedom within.

If your heart were right, then every created thing would be a mirror of life for you and a book of holy teaching, for there is no creature so small and worthless that it does not show forth the goodness of God. If inwardly you were good and pure, you would see all things clearly and understand them rightly, for a pure heart penetrates to heaven and hell, and as a man is within, so he judges what is without. If there be joy in the world, the pure of heart certainly possess it; and if there be anguish and affliction anywhere, an evil conscience knows it too well.

As iron cast into fire loses its rust and becomes glowing white, so he who turns completely to God is stripped of his sluggishness and changed into a new man. When a man begins to grow lax, he fears a little toil and welcomes external comfort, but when he begins perfectly to conquer himself and to walk bravely in the ways of God, then he thinks those things less difficult which he thought so hard before.

For Reflection

1. What does the author say about wealth, status, and beauty? From whom do our "natural gifts" come?

2. "If God were the sole object of our desire," Thomas says, we would not "be disturbed so easily by opposition to our opinions." Why not? How can focusing on God in our decision making help us to worry less about what others think of us? Do you agree or disagree?

3. What two "wings" does the author say lift us "up from the earth"? Describe each in your own words.

4. Choose one saying that you like from these excerpts. Explain the saying, and briefly describe its relevance to your life.

16 Hospitality of Heart

Introduction

Thrust into the skies of New York City's harbor is the welcoming torch of the Statue of Liberty. The poem inscribed at the statue's base, "The New Colossus," by Emma Lazarus, reminds us what true hospitality is:

> Give me your tired, your poor,
> Your huddled masses yearning to breathe free,
> The wretched refuse of your teeming shore.
> Send these, the homeless, tempest-tost to me,
> I lift my lamp beside the golden door!

In part because of this poem, Lady Liberty has long been an international icon teaching us to offer heartfelt hospitality to those in need.

Hospitality is a moral issue that goes hand in hand with Christian discipleship. In a Christian context, the lamp of the Statue of Liberty can symbolize the light of Christ welcoming all to the golden door of God's heart. Earlier in this reader, you have read how we are made in the image of God. As images of God, we are called to reflect his light and open our hearts to the needs of others—to see and respond to the image of Christ in others. To be a disciple of Christ is to respond to the gift of God's light and love by extending that gift to our fellow human beings in turn. In the Gospel of Matthew (25:35–36), Jesus describes the seven corporal works of mercy, charitable and hospitable actions that exemplify Christian discipleship by responding to people's physical needs and showing respect for human dignity. These works of mercy include feeding the hungry, giving drink to the thirsty, clothing the naked, sheltering the homeless, visiting the sick, visiting prisoners, and burying the dead. As we do for others, we do for Christ.

This chapter's selection is a 1945 column from *The Catholic Worker* newspaper, written by Dorothy Day (1897–1980), another icon of hospitality—one who embodied the corporal works of mercy as a disciple of Christ. Day, a convert to Catholicism and a social activist, was working as a journalist in the 1930s when the Great Depression took a severe toll on the United States. While writing a 1932 newspaper story on a hunger march in Washington, D.C., she was profoundly moved by those who were protesting. Seeing in them the suffering of Christ, she fervently prayed that God would show her a way to help the oppressed. His light had led her from agnosticism into Catholicism, and now she desired to live out her faith by serving the poor.

In her hometown of New York City—particularly hard hit by the Depression—she joined Peter Maurin to found *The Catholic Worker,* a newspaper that promoted Catholic social teachings rooted in the justice and charity of Jesus Christ. Soon Day and Maurin realized that the paper should not merely write about the plight of the poor—it should also take action by providing direct aid for those in need. Within months, Day and Maurin founded the first Catholic Worker movement house of hospitality in the slums of New York City. Christ, in the face of the poor and homeless, would be welcomed with a meal and a place to sleep. Today, houses of hospitality can still be found throughout the United States, and *The Catholic Worker* continues to be published.

In the reading here, written for Christmas in 1945, Day recalls the welcome the Christ Child received from the shepherds and the wise men at his birth, as well as the hospitality Jesus found in the homes of strangers and friends alike during his adult ministry. She reminds us that we show kindness to Christ in our own time whenever we show it to anyone in need—because we are all made in his image. "Christ is always with us," she says, "always asking for room in our hearts." How much simpler would

> " *Christ is always with us, always asking for room in our hearts.* "

the moral choices of life be if, in her words, "we forced ourselves to see that everywhere we go is Christ"?

"Room for Christ," in *The Catholic Worker* (December 1945)

By Dorothy Day

It is no use to say that we are born two thousand years too late to give room to Christ. Nor will those who live at the end of the world have been born too late. Christ is always with us, always asking for room in our hearts.

But now it is with the voice of our contemporaries that he speaks, with the eyes of store clerks, factory workers and children that he gazes; with the hands of office workers, slum dwellers and suburban housewives that he gives. It is with the feet of soldiers and tramps that he walks, and with the heart of anyone in need that he longs for shelter. And giving shelter or food to anyone who asks for it, or needs it, is giving it to Christ.

We can do now what those who knew Him in the days of His flesh did. I'm sure that the shepherds did not adore and then go away to leave Mary and her Child in the stable, but somehow found them room, even though what they had to offer might have been primitive enough. All that the friends of Christ did in His life-time for Him we can do. Peter's mother-in-law hastened to cook a meal for Him, and if anything in the Gospels can be inferred, it is surely that she gave the very best she had, with no thought of extravagance. Matthew made a feast for Him and invited the whole town, so that the house was in an uproar of enjoyment, and the straight-laced Pharisees—the good people—were scandalized. So did Zacchaeus, only this time Christ invited Himself and sent Zacchaeus home to get things ready. The people of Samaria, despised and isolated, were overjoyed to give Him hospitality, and for days He walked and ate and slept among them. And the loveliest of all relationships in Christ's life, after His relationship with his Mother, is His friendship with Martha, Mary and Lazarus and the continual hospitality He found with them—for there was always a bed for Him there, always a welcome, always a meal.

It is a staggering thought that there were once two sisters and a brother whom Jesus looked on almost as His family and where He found a second home, where Martha got on with her work, bustling round in her house-proud way, and Mary simply sat in silence with Him.

If we hadn't got Christ's own words for it, it would seem raving lunacy to believe that if I offer a bed and food and hospitality for Christmas—or any other time, for that matter—to some man, woman or child, I am replaying the part of Lazarus or Martha or Mary and that my guest is Christ. There is nothing to show it, perhaps. There are no haloes already glowing round their heads—at least none that human eyes can see. It is not likely that I shall be **vouchsafed** the vision of **Elizabeth of Hungary**, who put the leper in her bed and later, going to tend him, saw no longer the leper's stricken face, but the face of Christ. The part of a **Peter Claver**, who gave a stricken Negro his bed and slept on the floor at his side, is more likely to be ours. For Peter Claver never saw anything with his bodily eyes except the exhausted black faces of the Negroes. He had only faith in Christ's own words that these people were Christ. And when the Negroes he had induced to help him once ran from the room, panicstricken before the disgusting sight of some sickness, he was astonished. "You mustn't go," he said, and you can still hear his surprise that anyone could forget such a truth; "You mustn't leave him—it is Christ."

Some time ago I saw the death notice of a sergeant-pilot who had been killed on active service. After the usual information, a message was added which, I imagine, is likely to be imitated. It said that anyone who had ever known the dead boy would always be sure of a welcome at his parents' home. So, even now that the war is over, the father and mother will go on taking in strangers for the simple reason that they will be reminded of their dead son by the friends he made.

vouchsafed Granted or given as a favor.

Saint Elizabeth of Hungary (1207–1231) Daughter of the king of Hungary who rejected a life of luxury and dedicated herself to caring for the poor and suffering; patroness of Catholic charities. Her feast day is November 17.

Saint Peter Claver (1581–1654) Jesuit priest who ministered to the slaves of Colombia, assuring them of their human dignity and God's love for them; his feast day is September 9.

That is rather like the custom that existed among the first generations of Christians, when faith was a bright fire that warmed more than those who kept it burning. In every house then a room was kept ready for any stranger who might ask for shelter; it was even called "the strangers' room": and this not because these people, like the parents of the dead airman, thought they could trace something of someone they loved in the stranger who used it, not because the man or woman to whom they gave shelter reminded them of Christ, but because—plain and simple and stupendous fact—he was Christ.

It would be foolish to pretend that it is easy always to remember this. If everyone were holy and handsome, with **"alter Christus"** shining in neon lighting from them, it would be easy to see Christ in everyone. If Mary had appeared in Bethlehem clothed, as St. John says, with the sun, a crown of twelve stars on her head and the moon under her feet, then people would have fought to make room for her. But that was not God's way for her nor is it Christ's way for Himself now when He is disguised under every type of humanity that treads the earth.

To see how far one realizes this, it is a good thing to ask honestly what you would do, or have done, when a beggar asked at your house for food. Would you—or did you—give it on an old cracked plate, thinking that was good enough? Do you think that Martha and Mary thought that the old and chipped dish was good for their guest?

In Christ's human life there were always a few who made up for the neglect of the crowd.

The shepherds did it, their hurrying to the crib atoned for the people who would flee from Christ.

The wise men did it; their journey across the world made up for those who refused to stir one hand's breadth from the routine of their lives to go to Christ. Even the gifts that the wise men brought have in themselves an obscure recompense and **atonement** for what would follow later in this Child's life. For they brought gold, the king's

alter Christus Latin phrase meaning "another Christ."

atonement Process of making up for something; restoration, reparation, or compensation. Sometimes expressed as "at-one-with."

emblem, to make up for the crown of thorns that He would wear; they offered incense, the symbol of praise, to make up for the mockery and the spitting; they gave Him myrrh, to heal and soothe, and He was wounded from head to foot and no one bathed his wounds. The women at the foot of the cross did it too, making up for the crowd who stood by and sneered.

We can do it too, exactly as they did. We are not born too late. We do it by seeing Christ and serving Christ in friends and strangers, in everyone we come in contact with. While almost no one is unable to give some hospitality or help to others, those for whom it is really impossible are not debarred from giving room to Christ, because, to take the simplest of examples, in those they live with or work with is Christ disguised. All our life is bound up with other people; for almost all of us happiness and unhappiness are conditioned by our relationship with other people. What a simplification of life it would be if we forced ourselves to see that everywhere we go is Christ, wearing out socks we have to darn, eating the food we have to cook, laughing with us, silent with us, sleeping with us.

All this can be proved, if proof is needed, by the doctrines of the Church. We can talk about Christ's Mystical Body, about the vine and the branches, about the Communion of Saints. But Christ Himself has proved it for us, and no one has to go further than that. For He said that a glass of water given to a beggar was given to Him. He made heaven hinge on the way we act towards Him in his disguise of commonplace, frail and ordinary human beings. . . .

And to those who say, aghast, that they never had a chance to do such a thing, that they lived two thousand years too late, he will say again what they had the chance of knowing all their lives, that if these things were done for the very least of his brethren they were done for Him.

> **Mystical Body of Christ**
>
> The Mystical Body of Christ is the unity of all Christians with Christ in the Church. By the power of the Holy Spirit, each member is connected to the other members. Jesus taught us about this unity: "Whatever you did for one of these least brothers of mine, you did for me" (Matthew 25:40). Saint Paul also explores this: "There may be no division in the body. . . . If [one] part suffers, all the parts suffer with it; if one part is honored, all the parts share its joy" (1 Corinthians 12:25–26).

For a total Christian the **goad** of duty is not needed—always prodding him to perform this or that good deed. It is not a duty to help Christ, it is a privilege. Is it likely that Martha and Mary sat back and considered that they had done all that was expected of them—is it likely that Peter's mother-in-law grudgingly served the chicken she had meant to keep till Sunday because she thought it was "her duty"? She did it gladly: she would have served ten chickens if she had them.

If that is the way they gave hospitality to Christ, it is certain that is the way it should still be given. Not for the sake of humanity. Not because it might be Christ who stays with us, comes to see us, takes up our time. Not because these people remind us of Christ, as those soldiers and airmen remind the parents of their son, but because they are Christ, asking us to find room for Him exactly as He did at the first Christmas.

For Reflection

> **goad** Something that prompts one to take action; originally referred to a stick used for prodding animals.

1. This reading reminds us of the many people who offered hospitality to Jesus. Which biblical figures does Day describe? What are some opportunities for us to make room for Christ today, just as those people did two thousand years ago?

2. Reread the details about Saints Elizabeth of Hungary and Peter Claver. What common element does Day find in their stories? What does she want us to learn from them?

3. What gifts did the wise men bring to Bethlehem? According to Day, how did each gift atone for what followed in Christ's life? Explain the relevance of each gift in your own words.

4. Day says, "For a total Christian the goad of duty is not needed." Why not? Do you agree or disagree? Explain your response.

17 Virtue's Victory

Introduction

Can you think of a classic tale about a battle between good and evil? Perhaps you saw such a theme in a movie, or maybe a tale you were told in childhood stayed with you. Now think about the story you remember—what characteristics did its hero have? Humble? Courageous? Perhaps compassionate and loving? What were the negative qualities of the villain in your story? Proud? Deceitful? Envious?

The good qualities and habits a person possesses are called virtues. The opposite habits, ones that lead a person to sin, are called vices. Many stories of virtue versus vice show the conflict as an external one, taking place between two people or opposing groups. But each of us carries that moral conflict inside us. God created us in his image, one of love and holiness; yet as a result of Original Sin, we also are born with an internal struggle between virtuous choices and sinful choices. Though Jesus conquered sin, and though Original Sin is erased through Baptism, we continue to live with this ongoing internal conflict as a consequence of our first parents' sin.

The following selection is a morality play on the virtues written by a Benedictine abbess and German mystic, Hildegard of Bingen (1098–1179). The excerpt comes from *Scivias*, her written account of twenty-six visions that she had from God and her explanation of their meanings. In *Scivias* she summarizes many Christian teachings. The title is short for the Latin phrase *Scito vias Domini*—know the ways of the Lord. This reading's morality play about the virtues is an **allegorical** tale that Hildegard wrote to explain one of her visions.

Hildegard was a remarkable woman who was well ahead of her time. She could read and write, although few women of that period could do so; and her written works covered a broad range of subjects, including medicine, natural history, and theology. She also composed music. The play you will read in this chapter inspired her to write a longer version, called *Ordo Virtutum*, for which she also wrote the musical score. *Ordo Virtutum* (including this early version) is believed to be the first morality play. A literary form popular in the Middle Ages in Europe, a morality play was an allegorical story that personified the struggle between good and evil. The battlefield of the story was usually the human **soul**. The lessons on living a good life were both instructive and entertaining.

Some biblical review is helpful when interpreting the allegorical meaning of the reading in this chapter. Prompted by three ideas from *Scivias*, test your biblical knowledge with three questions: (1) Who could be called "the deceiver" in the first few chapters of the Bible? (2) Who is the King of Kings, as described in the last book of the Bible? (3) What are the "blessed mansions" that Hildegard mentions? The answers can be found in Genesis, chapter 3, Revelation 19:16, and John 14:2–3. Hildegard, writing for twelfth-century Catholics, assumes that the audience for this play is familiar with these and other allusions she makes to the Bible.

The very first morality narrative in the Bible is that of Adam and Eve. But this is no mere story. Rather, this account provides a framework for understanding our own internal battle: our creation in God's image, as well as our struggle with sin and vice as a result of the Fall of our first parents. Humans are created with free will, in the image and likeness of God, and we are animated—given

allegorical Referring to a literary form in which something is said to be like something else, in an attempt to communicate a hidden or symbolic meaning.

soul From the Latin word *anima*, which means life and breath; our spiritual principle, it is immortal, and it is what makes us most like God. Our soul is created by God. It is the seat of human consciousness and freedom.

Devil The fallen angel or spirit of evil who is the enemy of God and a continuing instigator of temptation and sin in the world.

souls—through God's love. Free will allows us to say yes to God, yes to virtue—but it means we are equally free to say yes to vice and sinful living. A war is being waged in our souls. To what, to whom, do we say yes?

In a theatrical way, Hildegard is telling us to say yes to virtuous living. As our souls struggle on the journey to our heavenly home, the virtues are our warriors in the battle against the forces of vice and the **Devil**. In the excerpt these virtues, acting as characters in the play, call upon the King of Kings to "guide your children with a favorable wind on the waters, that we may lead them into the celestial Jerusalem." Through biblical and sacramental imagery, Hildegard teaches us that victory awaits the virtuous soul.

Excerpt from *Scivias*

By Hildegard of Bingen

And again a song was heard, like the voice of a multitude, exhorting the virtues to help humanity and oppose the inimical arts of the Devil. And the virtues overcame the vices, and by divine inspiration people turned back to repentance. And thus the song resounded in harmony:

9. The exhortation of the virtues and the fight against the Devil

THE VIRTUES: We virtues are in God, and there abide; we wage war for the King of Kings, and separate evil from good. We appeared in the first battle, and conquered there, while the one who tried to fly above himself fell. So let us now wage war and help those who invoke us; let us tread underfoot the Devil's arts, and guide those who would imitate us to the blessed mansions.

SOULS (in the body, lamenting): Oh, we are strangers, wandering off toward sin! What have we done? We should have been daughters of the King, but we fell into the darkness of sin. O living Sun, carry us on Your shoulders into the just inheritance, which we lost in Adam! O King of Kings, let us fight in your battle!

A FAITHFUL SOUL: O sweet Divinity and O lovely Life, in Whom I may put on a robe of glory, and receive what I lost in the beginning! I long for You, and I call upon the virtues.

VIRTUES (answering): O blessed soul! O sweet creature of God, who were formed in the depths of God's profound wisdom, you have loved much.

THE SOUL: Oh, I come to you gladly; give me the kiss of the heart!

> **The *Protoevangelium***
>
> The first good news in the Bible is found in Genesis 3:15. This *protoevangelium*—a Latin word meaning "first gospel"—follows the story of the deceptive serpent's temptation of Adam and Eve and their prideful fall from grace. The serpent and sin, however, do not have the last word. Rather, in the very first chapters of the Bible, God promises ongoing opposition to evil, which will culminate in the definitive defeat of sin and death through the redemptive love of Jesus Christ.

VIRTUES: We must join with you in the battle, O daughter of the King.

THE SOUL (burdened and complaining): Oh, burdensome labor! Oh, heavy load I must endure while garbed in this life! It is most hard for me to fight against the flesh.

VIRTUES: O soul created by God's will, O happy instrument! Why are you so weak against the thing God has crushed by the Virgin? Through us you must conquer the Devil. . . .

KNOWLEDGE OF GOD: See what it is that you are clothed with, O daughter of salvation, and stand firm! Then you will never fall.

THE SOUL: Oh, I know not what to do or where to flee! Woe is me! I cannot use rightly that which clothes me. I want to tear it off!

VIRTUES: O bad conscience, O wretched soul! Why do you hide your face in the presence of your Creator?

KNOWLEDGE OF GOD: You do not know or see or taste Him Who created you.

THE SOUL: God created the world; I do Him no wrong if I want to enjoy it.

THE DEVIL (whispering to the soul): Fool, fool! What good is your labor? Regard the world, and it will embrace you with honor.

VIRTUES: Alas, alas! Virtues, let us loudly lament and mourn; for a sheep of the Lord is fleeing from life.

HUMILITY: I, Humility, queen of the virtues, say: Come to me, all of you virtues, and I will strengthen you, so that you can seek the lost coin and give it the crown of blessed perseverance!

VIRTUES: O glorious queen, O sweetest **mediator**! We come gladly.

HUMILITY: Beloved daughters, I keep you in the King's wedding chamber. O daughters of Israel, God raised you under His tree, so now remember your planting. Rejoice, O daughters of Zion!

THE DEVIL (to the virtues): What good is it that there should be no power but God's? I say that I will give everything to the one who follows me and his own will; but you and all your followers have nothing to give, for none of you knows who you are.

HUMILITY: I and my companions know well that you are the ancient dragon, who tried to fly higher than the Most High, and was thrown into the deepest abyss by God Himself.

VIRTUES: But all of us dwell on high.

THE SOUL (in the body, repentant and lamenting): O royal virtues! How beautifully you shine in the Supreme Sun! How sweet is your dwelling! Oh, woe is me, I fled from you!

VIRTUES: Come, O fugitive, come to us! and God will receive you.

THE SOUL: Alas, alas! Burning sweetness plunged

mediator One who facilitates agreement between conflicting parties; a reconciler or peacemaker.

me into sins; I dare not enter with you.

VIRTUES: Do not fear or flee; the Good Shepherd seeks you, His lost sheep.

THE SOUL: Now I need you to take me back, for I fester with wounds the ancient serpent has dealt me.

VIRTUES: Run to us, and follow with us that path in which you will never fall; and God will heal you.

THE SOUL: I am a sinner who fled from Life; I must come to you full of sores, that you may offer me the shield of redemption.

VIRTUES: O fugitive soul, be firm, and put on yourself the armor of light!

THE SOUL: O soldiery of the Queen. . . . I have lived as a stranger and an exile from you; help me to rise up in the blood of the Son of God! O Humility, who are true healing, help me; for Pride has broken me with many vices, and wounded me with many scars. Now I fly to you; oh, receive me!

HUMILITY (to the virtues): O virtues all, for the sake of Christ's wounds receive this mourning sinner, scarred as she is, and bring her to me.

VIRTUES (to the soul): We will bring you back, and we will not desert you; the whole celestial army rejoices over you! And so we will sing a song of rejoicing.

HUMILITY (to the soul): O unhappy daughter, I will embrace you; for the great Physician for your sake suffered deep and bitter wounds.

THE DEVIL (whispering to the soul): Who are you, and whence do you come? You embraced me, and I led you forth; and now you return and confound me! But I will throw you down in battle.

THE SOUL (to the Devil): I recognized that all your ways are evil, and so I fled from you. And now, O impostor, I fight against you! (To Humility): O Queen Humility, help me with your healing remedy!

HUMILITY (to Victory and the other virtues): O Victory! You conquered the Devil in Heaven; run now with your companions, and all bind this Devil!

VICTORY (to the virtues): O strong and glorious soldiers, come and help me conquer this deceiver!

VIRTUES (to Victory): O sweetest warrior in the flowing fountain that engulfed the ravenous wolf! O you crowned with glory, we gladly fight with you against the deluder of souls.

HUMILITY: Bind him, O splendid virtues!

VIRTUES: O queen, we will obey you, and do your commands in all things.

VICTORY: Rejoice, comrades! The ancient serpent is bound!

VIRTUES: Praise be to you, O Christ, King of the angels! O God, Who are You Who had this great counsel in You? It destroyed the hellish drink, which poisoned the publicans and sinners; and they now shine in celestial goodness. Praise therefore be to You, O King! O Father Almighty, from Your ardent heat flows the fountain; guide your children with a favorable wind on the waters, that we may lead them into the celestial Jerusalem.

For Reflection

1. In this reading from *Scivias,* what virtue does Hildegard consider to be the queen of virtues? What places it above all other virtues?

2. Hildegard describes the Soul as festering with sores inflicted by the ancient serpent. Who brings healing in this scene, and how does this healing happen?

3. Who or what are the "strong and glorious soldiers" that the character of Victory calls forth? Whom does Victory seem to represent?

4. How is the Sacrament of Baptism represented in this play?

18 A Spirit of Discretion

Introduction

> Thy friend has a friend, and thy friend's friend has a friend; be discreet.

> —*The Talmud: Selections*

What does it mean to be discreet? Why does this pithy piece of Jewish wisdom advise discretion? How could you apply this advice to your life?

This advice comes from the Talmud, an important text in Judaism that provides advice and instruction on Jewish law and ethics. Having been raised in a large Jewish family in Germany, Edith Stein (1891–1942) may have been familiar with Talmudic sayings such as this one about discretion. Discretion can be understood as an attitude that we should cultivate and practice in everyday life, such as when we are inclined to tell someone a secret. But discretion also plays a role in our response to the universal call to holiness. In this chapter's selection, "Discerning God's Designs," Stein distinguishes between discretion as a "natural disposition" and genuine discretion, which is made possible by the Holy Spirit.

Stein was raised in the Jewish faith, but in her teens she denied the existence of a personal God and professed atheism. She embarked on a profound quest for truth during her university studies and earned a doctorate in philosophy, one of the first women in Germany to do so. But the Holy Spirit was discreetly working in Stein's life. One night she stayed up to read the autobiography of Saint Teresa of Ávila, the great Carmelite reformer of the sixteenth century. The following morning she declared that she had found the truth. At age thirty-one she converted to Catholicism and sought to serve God through her philosophical work. Her writings fill seventeen volumes.

> **Discretion belongs essentially to each of the gifts: indeed, one could say that the Seven Gifts are varying expressions of this gift.**

Ten years later, in 1933, she entered the Carmelite order and became Sister Teresa Benedicta of the Cross. Sadly, the suffering of Christ on the cross awaited her. During World War II, she was living in the Netherlands when the Nazis rounded up Catholics and Jews alike. She was among the many arrested by the Gestapo and was deported to the Auschwitz concentration camp. There she died in its gas chamber, bearing witness to the truth.

The Spirit of truth guided Stein as she worked to discern God's design for her life. As she explains in this reading, the Christian moral life is one of **discernment**, the ongoing process of choosing the right thing to do, the right words to say, the right direction to follow—and above all, how God is calling us to spend our lives. But we are not left on our own in this process. Stein reassures us that the Holy Spirit inspires and impels us to think, speak, and act discreetly.

God has a providential design for our lives, enabled by the seven Gifts of the Holy Spirit: wisdom, understanding, counsel (right judgment), fortitude (courage), knowledge, piety (reverence), and fear of the Lord (wonder and awe). The seven Gifts of the Holy Spirit appear in the Old Testament, where the Book of Isaiah (11:2–3) describes them as gifts that the Messiah, the Christ, would possess in fullness. Through the power of the Holy Spirit, all Christians possess these gifts too. Stein explains why discretion is not listed among these gifts: "Discretion belongs essentially to each of the gifts: indeed, one could say that the Seven Gifts are varying expressions of this gift." This *sancta discretio*, or holy discretion, "can be found only where the Holy Spirit reigns."

discernment From a Latin word meaning "to separate or to distinguish between," it is the practice of listening for God's call in our lives and distinguishing between good and bad choices.

Excerpt from "Discerning God's Designs," from *Ganzheitliches Leben* [Holistic Life]

By Edith Stein (Saint Teresa Benedicta of the Cross, OCD)

The *Rule* of St. Benedict is called *discretione perspicua*, that is, distinguished by discretion. Discretion serves as a distinctive seal of Benedictine holiness. But fundamentally there is no holiness at all without it; indeed, if one grasps it with enough depth and breadth it becomes the same as holiness.

One entrusts a person with something "under discretion," that is, one expects silence to be kept about it. But discretion is more than keeping silence. A discreet person knows, without being requested to do so, when to refrain from speaking about something. He has the gift to *distinguish* between what must be kept in confidence and what must be revealed; when it is time to speak and when to be silent; to *whom* one may entrust something, to whom one may not. All this applies to his own affairs as well those of others. We do, after all, consider it an *indiscretion* if someone speaks about something concerning himself when it is untimely to do so, or when it would be harmful not to mention it.

One is handed a sum (of money) *at discretion,* that is, to be handled at our discretion. This does not imply we are to dispose of it at will. The donor has left us the choice of its application out of the conviction that we are most capable of deciding what should be done with it. In this case, too, discretion signifies a gift of discernment.

One who is to lead souls requires discretion to an exceptional degree. St. Benedict speaks of it

> **Rule of Saint Benedict**
>
> In the late fifth or early sixth century, Saint Benedict left the immorality of Rome to live as a hermit in the mountainous region of Subiaco in present-day Italy. His holiness attracted followers, and eventually a community formed that was known for its hospitality and its life of prayer and work; *ora et labora* is the Benedictine motto. Benedict wrote a rule—a constitution, or set of directives, for living in community—which the Benedictine community and many others still use today.

when he enumerates what is required of the abbot (*Rule,* chap. 64). He should exercise "foresight and consideration," and distinguish whether he is imposing a divine or a worldly task; he is to *discern* and exercise judgment, mindful of Jacob's decision when he said: "If I demand too much from my herd on the way, they shall all die within a single day" (Gen. 33:13). This and other manifestations of *discernment,* the mother of virtues, the abbot should take to heart, weighing all things so as to attain that which the **magnanimous** require and from which the weak will not recoil in fright. One might render *discretio* here as "wise moderation." But the source of such wise moderation is, after all, the gift to discern what is to be required from every single person.

Where do we obtain this gift? To a certain degree, there is a natural disposition for it. This we call tact, or sensitivity, the fruit of an inherited spiritual culture and of wisdom which has been assimilated after much education and life experience. Cardinal Newman says that the perfect gentleman resembles the saint enough to be mistaken for one. But that can be so only until a certain test of strength occurs. Beyond this limit, such natural equanimity breaks down. Nor does natural discretion **plumb** any depths. True, this type of discretion knows how to "get along with people" and can function like machine oil lubricating the wheels of life in society. But the thoughts of the heart, the deep interior of the soul, remain hidden from it. Only the spirit penetrates that far, that Spirit who searches out all things, even the depths of divinity.

Genuine discretion is supernatural. It can be found only where the Holy Spirit reigns, where a soul listens in total surrender and unhampered flexibility to the soft voice of its fair Guest and awaits his least nod.

Is *discretio* to be considered a gift of the Holy Spirit? It is not to be taken for one of the well-known Seven Gifts of the Holy Spirit, nor is it a new eighth one. Discretion belongs essentially to each of the gifts: indeed, one could say that the Seven Gifts are varying expressions of this gift. The gift of fear distinguishes in God his Divine Majesty (*divina maiestas*) and measures the

magnanimous Benevolent, generous, or big-hearted.

plumb To delve into, examine, or explore in depth.

infinite distance between God's holiness and one's own impurity. The gift of piety distinguishes in God the benevolence *(pietas)* of his Fatherhood and looks to him with filial, reverential love, with a love that knows how to discern what is due to the Father in heaven.

In the gift of counsel, it is most obvious that it is a gift of making distinctions—distinguishing in every life situation what is the proper thing to do. In fortitude, one might be inclined to think that we are dealing solely with the matter of the will. But a distinction between "counsel" that recognizes the right path without taking it and a "fortitude" that blindly insists on its own way is possible only in the purely natural sense. Where the Holy Spirit reigns, the human spirit becomes docile and submissive. Counsel calls for uninhibited practical behavior; fortitude is enlightened by counsel. Together, they offer flexibility to the human spirit so it can make fitting adaptations to conditions. Because it submits to the Holy Spirit without resistance, it is capable of meeting any situation it confronts. This heavenly light, as the gift of knowledge, allows one to discern in all clarity everything created, and all that happens, according to its relation with the eternal order, to understand its structure, and to allot it its fitting place and the importance which is its due. Yes, as the gift of understanding, it gives one insight into the depths of Divinity itself, and allows revealed truth to shine forth in all its fullness. In its perfection as the gift of wisdom, it unites one with the Triune God, permitting one to plumb the meaning of the eternal Source of all which emanates from it and which is sustained by him in that divine movement of life which is recognition and love combined.

Accordingly, *sancta discretio* differs radically from human cleverness. It does not differentiate by thinking through a matter step-by-step as does the researching human spirit, nor by dissecting and reconstructing, not by comparison and gathering, nor through concluding and proving. It discerns as effortlessly as the human eye distinguishes the sharp outlines of things in full daylight. Penetrating into details does not cause it to lose sight of the connections that are to be seen in a comprehensive view. The higher a wanderer climbs, the wider the range of vision becomes, until the full panoramic view at the summit bursts forth. The spiritual eye, enlightened by the heavenly light, peers to the farthest reaches, blurs nothing, renders nothing indistinguishable. With this unity, fullness increases until in a single ray of divine light the whole world becomes visible, as happened for St. Benedict in the *magna visio*.

For Reflection

1. What analogy does Stein use to illustrate natural discretion, the quality that allows us to "get along with people"? What are the merits of that kind of discretion? How is it different from genuine discretion, according to this reading?

2. Stein suggests that discretion plays a part in each of the seven Gifts of the Holy Spirit. Choose one of the seven gifts that she examines, and discuss how discretion is an expression of that gift.

3. Based on the reading, explain the difference between *sancta discretio* and cleverness.

4. In your own words, explain Stein's analogy of the wanderer climbing a mountain range as it relates to the concept of discretion.

19 The Primacy of Conscience

Introduction

At dawn on Tuesday, July 5, 1535, Sir Thomas More, former chancellor of England, was taken from his prison cell in the Tower of London to be executed for high treason. He was to die by means of beheading. By King Henry VIII's order, More was to be allowed only a few final words before his execution. On the scaffold, he succinctly stated, "I die the King's good servant, but God's first."

What act of treason did Saint Thomas More commit? He refused to take the oath of supremacy that would have required him to recognize the king, not the Pope, as the supreme head of the Church of England. The English parliament had issued the requirement at the king's request, partly in response to Pope Clement VII's denial of Henry's petition to annul his marriage to Catherine of Aragon. More's conscience dictated his decision. He could not swear allegiance to the king's authority in a way that placed the king above the spiritual authority of the Pope.

The first reading in this chapter contains excerpts from two letters that More wrote from his cell in the Tower of London: one that historians refer to as Letter 61, addressed to his daughter, Margaret; and the other, Letter 62, to a priest

> **Conscience**
>
> The *Catechism of the Catholic Church* describes conscience in the following way: "'Deep within his conscience man discovers a law which he has not laid upon himself but which he must obey. Its voice, ever calling him to love and to do what is good and to avoid evil, sounds in his heart at the right moment. . . . For man has in his heart a law inscribed by God. . . . His conscience is man's most secret core and his sanctuary. There he is alone with God whose voice echoes in his depths'[1]" (1776).

named Master Leder. Woven throughout are More's thoughts about the moral mandate to develop and pay attention to a well-formed conscience, even under pressure and threat of death. "I thank our Lord," he says, "that the thing that I do is not for obstinacy but for the salvation of my soul, because I cannot induce mine own mind otherwise to think than I do" (Letter 62). That is, he is not standing firm just to be stubborn; he is following his conscience for the sake of his own salvation.

The conscience is the "interior voice," guided by human reason and divine law, that leads us to understand ourselves as responsible for our actions and prompts us to do good and avoid evil. Each of us must form our conscience to be consistent with the divine inner voice, so that it can guide us to moral decisions. The Scriptures, Church teachings, the wisdom of saintly and holy people (alive and dead), prayer, and reflective reasoning are all means by which we can develop a well-formed conscience.

But living as our conscience dictates often is not easy. Moral actions may not always conform to society and its civil law, as was the case for More. But good moral choices always align with God's divine law inscribed on our hearts. As More explains to his daughter, each person has a duty, when facing a moral decision, to "examine his conscience surely by learning and by good counsel and be sure that his conscience be such as it may stand with [or support] his salvation"—or else "reform" the conscience (Letter 61).

More listened to his conscience and abided by its mandate, despite pressure from his king, the royal court, parliament, even his family and friends. As he tells Margaret here, he greatly feared the pain and death that awaited him. How did he not fold under such duress? He was a man of noble character, often called "a man for all seasons," a man who lived and died true to the voice of his conscience.

The second reading in this chapter is from Robert Bolt's twentieth-century play about More, titled *A Man for All Seasons*. In the scene you will read, More's daughter, Margaret (here called Meg), visits him in prison and tries to persuade him to save his life by taking the oath of supremacy. This scene illustrates More's integrity as he teaches Meg about the significance and solemnity of the words of an oath.

More's letters use sixteenth-century English language and spelling (explained in the notes and margins in this chapter), so these readings will require you to slow down and pay attention. They are worth your time. Thomas More was a man of immense intellect and integrity. He may have been writing for others, but you too can meet this man of conscience through his letters. His life witnesses even today to the primary importance of our conscience. As his character says in the play excerpt, "It's a matter of love."

Excerpts from *Letters from the Tower of London*

By Saint Thomas More

Letter 61

To Margaret Roper.
Tower of London
1534

THE HOLY SPIRIT OF GOD BE WITH YOU.
Your daughterly loving letter, my dearly beloved child, was and is, I faithfully assure you, much more inward comfort unto me than my pen can well express you, for **divers** things that I marked therein but of all things most especially, for that God of his high goodness giveth you the grace to consider the incomparable difference between the wretched estate of the present life and the wealthy state of the life to come. . . .

Surely Megge [Meg] a fainter heart than thy frail father hath, canst you not have. And yet I **verily** trust in the great mercy of God, that he shall of his goodness so stay[1] me with his holy hand that he

divers Various; archaic spelling of "diverse."

verily Truly.

shall not finally **suffer** me to fall wretchedly from his favor. And the like trust (dear daughter) in his high goodness I verily conceive of you. And so much the more, in that there is neither of us both, but that if we call his benefits to mind and give him oft thanks for them, we may find tokens[2] many, to give us good hope for all our manifold offenses toward him, that his great mercy, when we will heartily call therefor, shall not be withdrawn from us. And verily, my dear daughter, in this is my great comfort, that **albeit** I am of nature so shrinking from pain that I am almost afeard of a fillip,[3] yet in all the agonies that I have had, whereof before my coming hither (as I have showed you ere[4] this) I have had neither small nor few, with heavy fearful heart, forecasting all such perils and painful deaths, as by any manner of possibility might after fall unto me, and in such thought lain long restless and waking, while my wife had weened[5] I had slept, yet in any such fear and heavy pensiveness[6] (I thank the mighty mercy of God) I never in my mind intended to consent that I would for the enduring of the uttermost do any such thing as I should in mine own conscience (for with other men's I am not a man meet[7] to take upon me to meddle) think to be to myself, such as should damnably cast me in the displeasure of God. And this is the least point that any man may with his salvation come to, as far as I can see, and is **bounden** if he see peril to examine his conscience surely by learning and by good counsel and be sure that his conscience be such as it may stand with his salvation, or else reform it. And if the matter be such as both the parties may stand with salvation, then on whither[8] side his conscience fall, he is safe enough before God. But that mine own may stand with my own salvation, thereof I thank our Lord I am very sure. I beseech our Lord bring all parts[9] to his bliss. . . .

suffer Allow or permit.

albeit Although.

bounden Required, bound.

purpose Intend.

his Grace Title used for people of rank in the social order; here, refers to Henry VIII, the king of England.

Letter 62

To Master Leder.
Tower of London
Saturday
16 January 1534/5

. . . If my mind had been obstinate indeed I would not let[10] for any rebuke or worldly shame plainly to confess the truth. For I **purpose** not to depend upon the fame of the world. But I thank our Lord that the thing that I do is not for obstinacy but for the salvation of my soul, because I cannot induce mine own mind otherwise to think than I do concerning the oath [of supremacy].

As for other men's consciences, I will be no judge of, nor I never advised any man neither to swear nor to refuse, but as for mine own self if ever I should mishap[11] to receive the oath (which I trust our Lord shall never suffer me), ye may reckon sure that it were expressed and extorted by duresse and hard handling.[12] For as for all the goods of this world, I thank our Lord I set not much more by than I do by dust.[13] And I trust both that they will use no violent forcible ways, and also that if they would, God would of his grace and the rather a great deal

> " *My conscience knoweth God to whose order I commit the whole matter.* "

through good folks' prayers give me strength to stand. *Fidelis Deus* (saith Saint Paul) *qui non patitur vos tentari supra id quod potestis ferre, sed dat cum tentatione prouentum vt possitis sustinere* (1 Cor 10:13) ["God is faithful and will not let you be tried beyond your strength; but with the trial he will also provide a way out, so that you may be able to bear it"]. For this I am very sure, that if ever I should swear it [the oath], I should swear deadly against mine own conscience. For I am very sure in my mind that I shall never be able to change mine own conscience to the contrary; as for other men's, I will not meddle of.

. . . **His Grace** believeth me not that my conscience is the cause but rather obstinate willfulness. But surely that my let[14] is but my conscience, that knoweth God to whose order I commit the whole matter. *In cuius* *manu corda regum sunt* (Prov. 21:1) ["A king's heart is channeled water in the hand of the LORD"]. I beseech our Lord that all may prove as true faithful subjects to the King that have sworn as I am in my mind very sure that they be, which have refused to swear.

Endnotes

1. Support.
2. Signs of divine power.
3. Afraid of a small tap with the finger.
4. Before.
5. Thought.
6. Melancholy.
7. Fit.
8. Whichever.
9. Sides in the contention.
10. Refrain.
11. Have the misfortune.
12. More feared that he would be put to the torture.
13. Esteem them as worth no more than I do esteem dust.
14. Hindrance.

Excerpt from *A Man for All Seasons*

By Robert Bolt

MORE *(Looks at them, puzzled)* Well.

ROPER Sir, come out! Swear to the Act! Take the oath and come out!

MORE Is this why they let you come?

ROPER Yes . . . Meg's under oath to persuade you.

MORE *(Coldly)* That was silly, Meg. How did you come to do that?

MARGARET I wanted to!

MORE You want me to swear to the Act of Succession?

MARGARET "God more regards the thoughts of the heart than the words of the mouth." Or so you've always told me.

MORE Yes.

MARGARET Then say the words of the oath and in your heart think otherwise.

MORE What is an oath then but words we say to God?

MARGARET That's very **neat**.

MORE Do you mean it isn't true?

MARGARET No, it's true.

MORE Then it's a poor argument to call it "neat," Meg. When a man takes an oath, Meg, he's holding his own self in his own hands. Like water. *(He cups his hands)* And if he opens his fingers *then*—he needn't hope to find himself again. Some men aren't capable of this, but I'd be loathe to think your father one of them. . . . If we lived in a State where virtue was profitable, common sense would make us good, and greed would make us saintly. And we'd live like animals or angels in the happy land that *needs* no heroes. But since in fact we see that avarice, anger, envy, pride, sloth, lust and stupidity commonly profit far beyond humility, chastity, fortitude, justice and thought, and have to choose, to be human at all . . . why then perhaps we *must* stand fast a little—even at the risk of being heroes.

MARGARET *(Emotionally)* But in reason! Haven't you done as much as God can reasonably want?

MORE Well . . . finally . . . it isn't a matter of reason; finally it's a matter of love.

For Reflection

1. In his letter to Margaret, what does More say we are required to do if we see potential conflict and danger involving our conscience? How are we to do this?

2. Based on the letter to Master Leder, why is it so important to follow one's conscience? Why is it worth risking one's life?

3. In the play excerpt, the character of More compares swearing an oath to holding water. What does Bolt want us to understand about oaths and conscience, in light of this analogy?

20 Talking with Jesus

Introduction

There once was a bedridden old man near the end of his life. When his parish priest came to pray with him, the man confessed that he had never prayed much because he did not know how. The priest pulled an empty chair up to the man's bed and told him to imagine Jesus sitting there. "Talk with Jesus as a dear friend, and with your heart, listen to his response."

A few weeks later the man's daughter called the priest with news of her father's death. "You know, there was something unusual when Dad died," she added. "He was resting comfortably when I left the room, but when I returned, he had died peacefully. What was strange, though, was that he had leaned over and was resting his head on the empty chair next to his bed."

The priest in that story may well have read one of the many writings on prayer and the moral life by Saint Alphonsus de Liguori (1696–1787). The excerpt that you will read in this chapter is from Liguori's book titled *Conversing with God as a Friend*. A good definition of the moral life must include friendship with God. Any friendship is a relationship that develops over time

> **Prayer**
>
> Prayer is the lifting up of one's mind and heart to God. Prayer can take on different forms. Prayers of petition ask God for help; prayers of thanksgiving are just that—thanks given to God. Prayers of blessing ask for God's loving care for another person. Intercessory prayers ask for divine assistance for other people's needs; Saint Anthony, for example, is known for interceding for those who have lost something, but anyone can pray on behalf of another. Finally, prayers of praise acknowledge and affirm the greatness of God.

through conversations, correspondence, or shared experiences. No friendship, human or divine, is possible without communication and connection.

When it comes to friendship with God, communication and connection are called "prayer," and prayer is what opens our hearts to the abundant graces he sends us to guide moral living. Therefore, Liguori advises in this reading, "Accustom yourself to speak to God, one to one, in a familiar manner as to the dearest friend you have and who loves you best of all" (6). He explains that we should bring all our daily triumphs and concerns to God. And knowing that we sometimes find that difficult, Liguori reassures us that we invite God to be near us and to help us pray, simply through our desire to be in a loving relationship with him.

Liguori modeled and taught moral living by his life and work, rooted in prayer. His writings on moral theology have earned him the title of Doctor of the Church and made him the patron saint of moral theologians. Born to an affluent Italian family, Liguori was well educated, earning a double doctorate before going on to practice law. As a child he had received from his mother a handwritten prayer book, and through prayerful conversations with God, he ultimately felt called to abandon his law career to become a priest.

All around Liguori was great physical and spiritual poverty. He responded by forming lay groups that came together to pray, study the Catholic faith, visit Jesus in Eucharistic devotion, and practice acts of service and charity for others. Liguori preached in a down-to-earth way that invited people to lead moral lives based on a loving relationship with God. The religious order he founded, the Redemptorists, continues his work today through retreat centers and parish missions meant to provide personal, prayerful, and positive experiences of God's presence today.

Conversing with God as a Friend is Liguori's response to the rigorous morality of his day that prompted people to undertake prayer and devotional practices out of fear of God rather than in friendship with him. Liguori's teachings, as true today as they were in his time, tell us to talk with God and trust that he is listening and responding as a dear and affectionate friend.

Excerpt from *Conversing with God as a Friend*

By Saint Alphonsus de Liguori

6. Accustom yourself to speak to God, one to one, in a familiar manner as to the dearest friend you have and who loves you best of all. It is a great mistake to treat God with uncertainty and to enter God's presence like a slave who, ashamed and full of fear, comes trembling with terror into the presence of a prince. It is even a greater mistake to think that conversation with God is nothing but boredom and tediousness. Nothing could be farther from the truth. "For association with her involves no bitterness / and living with her no grief, / but rather joy and gladness" (Wis 8:16). Ask people who love God with a true love and they will tell you that in the troubles of their lives they have found no greater or more genuine relief than in loving conversation with God.

7. This loving conversation does not demand that you constantly strain your mind at the expense of your other activities or even your recreation. It only requires that, without neglecting your other obligations, you act on occasion toward God in the same way that you act toward those whom you love or who love you.

8. Your God is ever at your side, indeed, within you. "'In him we live and move and have our being'" (Acts 17:28). You don't need to work through a doorman if you want to approach God. God delights in your intimacy. Discuss all your business with God, your plans, your troubles, your fears—anything at all that concerns you. And do so with confidence, with your heart open wide. God can scarcely speak to the person who does not speak to God. Those who are not accustomed to speaking to God will scarcely recognize God's voice when he does speak. And so the Lord remarks with regret: "As far as love is concerned, our sister is but a child; how can I succeed in speaking to her if she isn't capable of understanding me?" ([ed.] Sg 8:8). When we despise God's gift, God might seem to us

to be a mighty and fearsome Lord. When we love God we find a most affectionate friend. That is why God desires to converse with us often—like a friend, without the slightest embarrassment.

9. It is true of course that we owe God the greatest reverence but when God makes his presence felt to you and makes known to you his desire that you speak to him as one who loves you above all else, then express your feelings with full freedom and trust. "He who watches for her at dawn shall not be disappointed, / for he shall find her sitting by his gate" (Wis 6:14). God doesn't even wait for you to take the first step. When you desire his love he leaps ahead and presents himself to you bringing with him the graces and gifts you most need. God waits for just a word from you to show you how near he is, how ready he is to hear and comfort you. "The LORD has eyes for the just / and ears for their cry" (Ps 34:16).

10. God by his immensity can be found everywhere but there are two places that are his home in a special way: One is in heaven in the glory which he shares with the blessed; the other is on earth, in the humble who love him. "I dwell . . . with the crushed and dejected in spirit" (Is 57:15). This then is our God: Dwelling in the highest heaven he does not consider it beneath him to spend night and day among his faithful ones in their caves and huts. He shares with them there his divine consolations which surpass the greatest pleasures the world can offer. Only the person who has not experienced this can fail to long for it. "Learn to savor how good the LORD is" (Ps 34:9).

11. Friends in the world have times when they speak together and times when they are apart: but between God and you there need not pass a second of separation, if that is your wish. "When you lie down, you need not be afraid, / when you rest, your sleep will be sweet. . . . / For the LORD will be your confidence" (Prv 3:24, 26). You may sleep and the Lord will place himself at your side and ever watch over

> **God waits for just a word from you to show you how near he is, how ready he is to hear and comfort you.**

you. . . . While you sleep he is as close as your pillow and he remains always thinking of you so that, if you happen to awaken in the night, he might speak to you with his inspirations and to hear from you some expression of love, of self-offering, of thanksgiving. Even in the hours of the night he does not want your loving and sweet conversation to be broken. Sometimes God may even speak to you as you sleep and cause you to hear his voice so that, on awaking, you may put your good inspirations into action. "In dreams will I speak" (Nm 12:6).

12. God awaits you in the morning to hear from you some word of affection or of trust; to receive from you your first thoughts, the promises of the actions which you will perform that day for his pleasure; and to hear of the sufferings that you will endure for the sake of his love and glory. God does not fail to be present to you from the moment you awaken; do not fail then, on your part, to give God a glance of love and rejoice to hear the joyful news that your God is not distant from you as he once may have been because of your sins. God loves you and wants nothing more than to be loved by you. From the first moment of the day he imposes on you the loving commandment: "You shall love the LORD, your God, with all your heart" (Dt 6:5).

13. Never forget the sweet presence of God, as do the majority of people. Talk to God as often as you can for he never tires of listening to you as do the great ones of this earth. If you truly love God, you will never lack for things to say to him. Tell him everything that happens to you; tell him about all your concerns just as you would to the dearest friend.

Don't treat him as if he were a self-impressed prince who only **deigns** to speak to the great and about great things. It delights our God to come down to our level and he is thrilled to hear from us about all our concerns, no matter how small they may appear to us. He loves us so much and takes as good care of you as if you were his only care in the world. God is so devoted to your interests; it

deigns Condescends to offer or do something, usually as a sign of favor shown by someone powerful to someone who is not.

Providence The guidance, material goods, and care provided by God that is sufficient to meet our needs.

omnipotence Absolute and unlimited power. One of the attributes of God; others are omniscience, or knowledge of everything; omnipresence, or presence everywhere; and omnibenevolence, or all-goodness.

is as if **Providence** existed only to aid you; **omnipotence** only to help you; the divine mercy and goodness only to sympathize with you, to do you good, to win your confidence by the delicacy of his affection. Open your inner world to God with perfect freedom and pray that he guide you to do his holy will perfectly. Let your every desire and plan be directed only to the discovery of God's good pleasure and to give joy to the divine heart. "Commit your way to the Lord" (Ps 37:5); "ask him to make all your paths straight and to grant success to all your endeavors and plans" (Tb 4:19).

14. Never say: What is the point of revealing all my wants to God since God sees them already and knows them better than I? God knows them all, but God acts as if he doesn't know whatever needs you experience about which you do not speak or seek his help. Our Savior knew well that Lazarus was dead but acted as if he didn't until he heard it from Mary Magdalene and then consoled her by returning her brother to life.

15. Whenever you are afflicted by some illness, temptation, persecution, or other problem, go at once to God so that his hand may reach out to help you. It is enough for you to present your trouble to him saying: "Look, Lord, upon my distress" (Lam 1:20). God will not fail to comfort you or at least to give you the strength to suffer the difficulty with patience. In that case, everything will turn out better for you than if he had released you from the difficulty. Tell God all about the thoughts of fear or depression that torment you and say: My God, in you is all my hope. I offer this trouble to you and I resign myself to your will; but please have pity on me. Either free me from this suffering or give me the strength to bear it. God will not fail to keep the promise made in the gospel to all those who suffer—to comfort and to strengthen all who come in search of help: "Come to me, all you who labor and are burdened, and I will give you rest" (Mt 11:28).

For Reflection

1. Liguori says, "Those who are not accustomed to speaking to God will scarcely recognize God's voice when he does speak." What does he mean?

2. According to Liguori, what two places are God's special home? In what way does God dwell in each home named in the excerpt?

3. Based on this reading, what loving command is imposed on you each day? How does it promote friendship with God? Describe two examples of ways you can personally respond to that command.

4. How are you to deal with "some illness, temptation, persecution, or other problem," according to Liguori? Have you felt God's strength help you to bear a suffering, or do you know someone who has? Describe the experience.

Part 4

Sin and Hope in the Redemptive Love of Christ

21 Disabling Vice and Enabling Virtue

Introduction

For many years at Saint Norbert College in De Pere, Wisconsin, students have gathered every Wednesday morning in an old church for a prayer service and presentation by members of the school community. When Paul Wadell, a professor of religious studies at the school, was invited to present, he chose the topic of hope. He began his talk with a story about the nineteenth-century Scottish novelist and poet Robert Louis Stevenson, who described the work of the men who lit the gas streetlamps as "punching holes in the darkness." In his talk Wadell used this as a metaphor: "When we hate what is evil and hold fast to what is good, . . . we punch holes in the darkness and give witness to the light."

This final part of the reader is titled "Sin and Hope in the Redemptive Love of Christ." Sin is any deliberate offense, in thought, word, or deed, against the will of God; it wounds human nature and injures human solidarity. But even though sin is real and present, we know it does not have the last word, thanks to our life in Christ. Christians need not remain in the darkness of sin, for we walk in the light of Christ. Like Stevenson's lamplighter, Jesus came and made holes in the darkness.

The excerpt for this chapter comes from Wadell's book *The Primacy of Love: An Introduction to the Ethics of Thomas Aquinas,* one of several books Wadell has written on moral theology and ethics, with a particular focus on virtue. The following reading is from his chapter called "The Virtues: Actions That Guide Us to Fullness of Life." The fullness of life is not achieved without struggle, Wadell explains, because every virtue seems to have an opposing vice. He contrasts some virtues with vices and helps us to understand the age-old question of "why it can be so difficult to change behavior" (p. 118). As the title of his book suggests, Wadell's starting point for understanding virtue and vice is the *Summa Theologica* of Saint Thomas Aquinas, a thirteenth-century Dominican philosopher and theologian and one of the Doctors of the Church. Wadell quotes Aquinas when he reassures us that sin can be overcome, for virtue not only helps us be better people but actually works to "gradually erode the opposing conditions" to goodness (p. 117).

The second reading comes from Aquinas's *Summa Theologica*, his great summary of theology. This passage is from the section that Wadell discusses in the first reading. *Summa Theologica* is not easy reading, but the morsel included here will allow you to begin exploring the classic work. In this excerpt, which examines the question of whether a single act is sufficient to build a habit (good or bad), Aquinas refers to the "appetitive power." In the most basic way, he is talking about our human will and the role it plays in helping us to develop habits of virtue.

Despite the nearly six hundred years between them, Wadell and Aquinas unite to reassure us that vice will lessen its hold as we grow in virtue, and they advise that by disabling vice we enable virtue. Hope is an essential Christian virtue—one of the theological virtues—but in the darkness of its shadow lies despair, the abandonment of all hope. We must not only be aware of the darkness of despair but also battle against it, making holes where hope can shine through.

Excerpt from *The Primacy of Love: An Introduction to the Ethics of Thomas Aquinas*

By Paul J. Wadell

Developing a Virtue Often Means Overcoming a Vice

A further reason acquiring virtue is difficult is that so often to develop a virtue means a vice must be overcome. Thomas [Aquinas] suggests this when he observes one reason it is hard to grow in virtue is that the will is turned "to many incompatible things" and thus virtue must work not only to imbue us with goodness, but also to "gradually erode the opposing conditions" of goodness (ST [*Summa Theologica*], I–II, 51,3). Those opposing conditions are many. It is our inclination to evil, it is the presence of unhealthy, destructive tendencies, it is the stubborn power of vices which resist the development of virtues. At least initially, the primary work of virtue may be the toilsome task of uprooting a vice. We need to develop good habits because we have bad habits of which we need to be rid. Virtues are habits which turn us to the good, but vices are habits too; they are bad habits which turn us away from goodness. Virtues are enabling, vices are disabling. Virtues upbuild us, vices corrupt us.

At first, the virtues work a rehabilitation, they struggle to heal a personality broken and wounded by debilitating behavior, and this may comprise a large portion of our moral history. If vice corrupts, virtue renovates, shaping us in goodness by first healing us from evil. Virtues do not work on virgin soil—they work to heal a personality already wounded by sin. It is not as if the virtues appear where nothing was before, for indeed most often acquiring a virtue means overcoming a contrary **disposition**. And this is not easy. Vices do not die easily, and the reason is that like the virtues they are habits, ingrained tendencies to act a certain way. Vices resist virtue. Because they are habits, they actively seek to overcome any opposing tendencies. We know this in our experience. One reason it is hard to develop patience is that being quick-tempered is a vice, and because it is a vice it is a predictable, firmly lodged way of acting. Or take generosity. Generosity is slowly gained where a stingy spirit once prevailed. Or forgiveness is only painstakingly had where one has been inclined to hardness of heart. These are all the "opposing conditions" to which Aquinas refers. Acquiring virtue takes time because so many vices must be dislodged. To establish virtue, good habits must overcome bad habits, and bad habits do not willingly die.

We may, for example, have a bad habit of gossiping, a bad habit of holding

disposition A tendency to act in a particular way; an inclination.

moral realism Acknowledgment that objective facts support a moral claim.

grudges, a bad habit of eating or drinking too much. These are all vices, ingrained, habitual ways of acting, and the longer they have characterized us the deeper in us they have grown. It is not easy to change bad behavior because vices are habits too; they enter us, they become part of our personality. If the quality of a good act passes over into us and leaves its mark, a quality of a bad act leaves its mark too. If virtue works, vice does too. Vice works to overcome and destroy virtue; it is the nature of a habit. Vices are entrenched, and struggle to survive because they are habits. They are not passive before virtue, they are active, fiercely opposing whatever works to silence them. For every virtue there is its opposite working to overcome it.

This helps us understand why it can be so difficult to change behavior, or why it is so maddeningly hard to uproot one habit for the sake of nurturing another one. It also explains why initially our virtue is flickering. In the early stages of its development, all virtue

> " *To grow in virtue is to be pried free of vice.* "

is in danger of being snuffed out by vices, and the reason is that the vices, because they are more firmly developed, are much more powerful than the virtues. If virtues are powers to do good, vices are powers to do evil. Vices resist virtues, they fight being overcome and destroyed by goodness. Vices struggle to survive, which is why we can be easily discouraged in the early stages of our moral development. There is much in us that must be burned away, purged and cleansed before virtue can flourish.

There is **moral realism** here. Thomas paints a picture of our lives locked in a struggle between good and evil. Each of us is a mixture of both. Morally speaking, a war is being waged in our hearts. It is a war between virtue and vice, a war to see which will prevail in us. We have a disposition to virtue, but we also have a disposition to vice. We develop some virtues, but we know we have developed vices as well. None of us is completely virtuous, but are at least partially controlled by vice. Aquinas's image is of a moral subject under fire. On the one hand, there are virtuous dispositions in us which empower our growth in the good; on the other hand, this progress in virtue is subverted by all those forces in us—Thomas calls them vices—which threaten to pull us down, discourage us, and finally destroy us. Vices work to **vitiate** the goodness we may have already attained, which is why the development of one bad habit usually signals the erosion of goodness elsewhere in our lives. The moral life stands in tension. To grow in virtue is to be pried free of vice. We stand somewhere in between, hopefully moving toward virtue, but feeling strongly the pull of vice.

The fact that virtue is acquired only with effort suggests that most often taking on a good habit means uprooting and destroying a bad one. Virtues move in where vices used to be. Justice works against selfishness, temperance against debasement, courage against cowardice and reckless-ness. We are a mix of tendencies, a blend of conflicting forces. Virtues always have opposites, and their opposites are the vices. Vices make virtues necessary, but they also help us understand why we sometimes feel so deeply a contradiction at the heart of our lives, a sort of interior division; even when we strive to be good, do we not still feel the power and hold of sin? It is not surprising then that we can be easily discouraged in our ef-forts to be good. Why is it that we sometimes are brought down by things we thought we had left behind? We find ourselves being petty or petulant and are surprised because we thought we had developed graciousness. The reason may be that all these negative qualities might be more deeply a part of us than we expected. If they were habitual enough to have become vices, their death will come slowly; and sometimes when we think they are finally purged from us they suddenly reassert themselves, which might explain why our sinfulness so often catches us off guard. These opposite tendencies are set deeply within us, and they are neither passive nor inert. As we grow in virtue we do lessen the hold of sin upon our lives, but if sin is a habit of being it is likely that some trace of it will survive.

vitiate To impair or make something less effective.

whence From which; from this point.

wherefore For this reason; therefore.

Excerpt from *Summa Theologica*

By Saint Thomas Aquinas

Question 51. The cause of habits, as to their formation

Article 3. Whether a habit can be caused by one act?

. . . Habit is caused by act, because a passive power is moved by an active principle. But in order that some quality be caused in that which is passive the active principle must entirely overcome the passive. **Whence** we see that because fire cannot at once overcome the combustible, it does not enkindle at once; but it gradually expels contrary dispositions, so that by overcoming it entirely, it may impress its likeness on it. Now it is clear that the active principle which is reason, cannot entirely overcome the appetitive power in one act: because the appetitive power is inclined variously, and to many things; while the reason judges in a single act, what should be willed in regard to various aspects and circumstances. **Wherefore** the appetitive power is not thereby entirely overcome, so as to be inclined like nature to the same thing, in the majority of cases; which inclination belongs to the habit of virtue. Therefore a habit of virtue cannot be caused by one act, but only by many.

> **Thomas Aquinas and Scholasticism**
>
> Scholasticism is a medieval method of critical thinking that follows strict forms of logical structure. Aquinas wrote his *Summa Theologica* in the scholastic style. Sometimes called the *Summa*, this three-volume work was meant as a summary of Christian theology. Shortly before he died, Aquinas was working on a *Summa of the Summa*—a shorter summary of the multiple volumes. But after a mystical experience that he never explained, he stopped writing, saying that what he had written seemed now "like straw."

For Reflection

1. According to Wadell what is the "primary work of virtue" at first? Provide a concrete example of this point.

2. Based on the reading by Wadell, explain why all virtue in its early stages is so easily extinguished. What does he suggest is the remedy?

3. Wadell writes that "virtues move in where vices used to be." What does he mean? What pairs of virtues and opposing vices does he name? Which of these virtues would you like to develop? Why?

4. Explain the fire analogy Aquinas gives in the *Summa Theologica*. What does this analogy illustrate about the development of virtue?

22 A Conversion of Heart

Introduction

Thump-thump . . . thump-thump . . . Can you feel the pulse of your blood? God stands at the door of your heart and knocks with each beat. The pulse of God's presence and the breath of God's Spirit point to the gift of life within you. But God's gift of grace awaits your response. Will you freely open your heart's door to welcome God and accept his divine gift, or will you turn away?

This chapter's selection comes from a memoir that has been called one of the greatest spiritual autobiographies ever written. *The Confessions* offers the recollections of the restless heart of Saint Augustine of Hippo (354–430), who for many years refused to open his heart to God's persistent presence. Augustine grew up in the Roman Empire, in the province of North Africa. He was the son of a pagan father, who took pride in his son's physical and intellectual abilities but was less concerned with his ethics and values. But Augustine's Christian mother, Monica, prayed and wept many tears for his conversion from sinful ways. Augustine received a classical education and became a professor of **rhetoric**. He entered a common-law marriage and fathered a child, yet his heart was restless and always searching.

Then the Christian teaching of his youth was brought to life by the brilliant rhetorician Saint Ambrose, who was then the bishop of Milan, where Augustine was teaching. Through Ambrose's preaching, Monica's prayers, and the power of God's grace, Augustine underwent a conversion of heart. He was baptized by Ambrose and later returned to North Africa, eventually becoming a priest and then the bishop of Hippo (in modern-day Algeria).

> **rhetoric** The examination or practice of the persuasive use of language; a classical field of study.

In his *Confessions* Augustine looks back and sees God's hidden presence through the events of his life. He addresses this book to God, the love of Augustine's life, but he says he has written it for us. In the first part of this reading, he describes how he turned away from the depth of divine grace and instead turned to sin. The excerpt includes details about Augustine's adolescent relationship with his parents and a well-known account of thievery. As one sinful act led to another, he explains, he found himself journeying further and further from God, weighed down and weakened by **concupiscence**, especially lust. But Augustine discovered that it is never too late to turn from a life of sin. In the second part of the reading, Augustine describes one moment in his conversion and the opening of his heart to God's ever-present grace.

Metanoia is a theological term meaning a change of heart, a turning away from one way of thinking and acting and toward another. The title of Augustine's autobiography, *The Confessions,* captures that idea of turning, both away from something and toward something else. The word *confession* has two meanings: an admission of wrongdoing but also an expression of belief. Augustine's *Confessions* embraces both meanings. It is a passionate and personal account of Augustine's turn from the depravation and sin in his life, and also his turn to the fullness of life in Christ. It is the story of the conversion of his heart.

Excerpts from *The Confessions*

By Saint Augustine of Hippo

Book Two

2.3.5. . . . To whom am I telling all this? It is not to you, my God; rather it is from within you that I speak to my own kind, to my fellow-men, however few may come to read these words of mine. And why do I do so? So that I and any reader of mine may reflect upon the depths from which we must call upon you. For what is closer to your ears than a heart that confesses you, and a life *lived by faith* (Habakkuk 2.4, Rom. 1.17,

Gal. 3.11). Everyone heaped praise upon my father because he spent beyond our family's resources to ensure that his son had everything he would need when he was pursuing his studies far from home. There were many

citizens far wealthier than we were who took no such trouble on behalf of their children. My father, for his part, was not so worried about what sort of man I was growing up to be in your sight, or how I kept my chastity. . . . I grew rank and untended by you, O God, the one true and good *Lord of your field* (Matt. 13.24–30), my heart.

2.3.6. So it was that in my sixteenth year . . . the brambles of lust grew up over my head, and there was no hand to uproot them. Indeed, when my proud father saw in the **public baths** that I was reaching puberty and had put on the restlessness of youth, he was as pleased as if I had already made him a grandfather; and, drunk with joy, he announced the news to my mother. Such is the way in which the world forgets its Creator and loves your creation instead of you (Rom. 1.24), drunk on the invisible wine of its own will, perverse as it is and bent on lower things. But within my mother's heart you had already established your Temple, and laid the foundations of your holy dwelling-place (1Cor. 1.16–17, Ecclesiasticus 24.14), while my father was still under instruction in the faith, and indeed had only recently begun it. My mother was full of holy fear and trembling (2Cor. 7.15); and though I was not yet a believer, she was afraid that I had already strayed into

Original Sin

Augustine helped to clarify the Church's doctrine of Original Sin. Original Sin was the sin of the first human beings, who disobeyed God's command by choosing to follow their own will and thus lost their original holiness and became subject to death. This fallen state of human nature affects every person born into the world. In his writings Augustine reflected on our human inclination to sin, both as individuals and as societies.

the tortuous paths walked by those who turn their back towards you and not their face (cf Jer. 2.27).

2.3.7. Do I venture to say that you, my God, kept silence all the time I was wandering further and further from you? Woe to me if I do. Was it thus that you were silent at that time? Whose words were they but yours that you whispered to me through your faithful servant, my mother? None of these counsels, however, sunk into my heart; I did not follow them. For she wanted me to avoid fornication, and most of all—and in some corner of my heart I remember how anxiously she admonished me—not to commit adultery. . . . You were speaking to me through her, and not keeping silent; and in despising my mother and *your maidservant,* I was despising you, *my Master* (Ps. 116.14 [Ps. 115.16]). But I did not know that it was your voice. So blind was I, and so precipitate was my fall, that when I heard my contemporaries boasting of their exploits, I felt ashamed that I had less to be ashamed of. The more immoral their actions, the more they would brag about them. They lusted for such acts, and not for the act alone; they lusted also for glory. What is worthy of **censure**, if not vice? I, however, was becoming more vicious in order to avoid censure. And when my actions were not enough to put me on a level with these hardened delinquents, I would pretend to have done things that I had not. I was afraid that the more innocent I was, the more of a coward I would seem; and that the more chaste I was, the more contemptible I would be considered. . . .

2.4.9. Theft, O Lord, is certainly punishable under both your Law and under the law that is written on the human heart, that sin itself cannot erase. No thief can endure another thief with equanimity, even if one is wealthy and the other is driven by poverty to crime. But it was not poverty that drove me to conceive the desire to steal, and to act upon that desire. I lacked only righteousness, and my stomach turned at it; I had grown fat on wickedness. What I stole, I already had in abundance, and of much better quality too. I did not steal so as to enjoy the fruits of my crime, but rather to enjoy the theft itself, and the sin.

censure A stern rebuke or expression of disapproval, often issued in public.

insalubrious Unhealthy in some respect; here, refers to unhealthy morals.

There was a pear tree in the orchard next to ours, laden with pears, but not ones especially appealing either to the eye or the tongue. At dead of night, after messing around on some empty plots in our usual **insalubrious** manner, a group of us young delinquents set out, our plan being to shake the tree and make off with the pears. We carried off a vast haul of them—but not in order to feast on them ourselves; instead, we meant to throw them to the pigs. And though we did eat some of them, we did so only for the pleasure we had in tasting forbidden fruit. Such was my heart,

> *Such is the way in which the world forgets its Creator and loves your creation instead of you.*

O God; such was my heart, on which you showed your pity in the depths of the abyss. Let my heart now tell you what its purpose was; why I was gratuitously evil, and why there was no reason for my evil save evil itself. My evil was loathsome, and I loved it; I was in love with my own ruin and rebellion. I did not love what I hoped to gain by rebellion; it was rebellion itself that I loved. Depraved in soul, I had leapt away from my firm foothold in you and cast myself to my destruction, seeking to gain nothing through my disgrace but disgrace alone. . . .

2.6.12. But you, my theft, the crime I committed that night of my sixteenth year—what was there in you that I was so wretched as to love? You had no beauty, being a theft. Are you indeed anything at all, that I can address you in this way? The pears that I stole were indeed beautiful, for you, O God, had created them; you, the creator of all things and of all things the most beautiful, the good God, the highest Good, my true Good. The pears were beautiful; but it was not them that my soul so pitiably desired. I had plenty of pears, and better ones too; the ones I picked, I picked only in order to steal. Once I had picked them, I threw them away; I feasted only on the wickedness that was the fruit of my theft. If any morsel of pear entered my mouth, it was the crime of stealing that gave it spice. And now, O Lord God, I would [like to] know what it was about the theft that gave me such delight. There was no beauty in it; not the beauty that we find in justice or in wisdom, nor the sort we find in the human mind, in our memory, our senses, or in the very pulse of life;

not even such as we see in the stars, each shining in its proper place, or in the earth or sea, teeming with life that is reborn as each generation passes. There was not even the appearance of beauty that vices possess, imperfect and shadow-like as it is; for vice always falls short of its aim.

2.6.13. Pride imitates exalted status, whereas you alone are exalted as God above all things. Ambition seeks nothing but honours and glory, whereas you alone are worthy of honour above all things, and your glory endures for ever. The savagery that waits on power seeks to be feared; but who should be feared save God alone, and who or what can ever strip him of his power or detract from it in any way? The sensualist seeks the charms of love; but there is no charm greater than your love, nor anything that we may more profitably love than your Truth, more lovely and radiant than all things. A shallow and inquisitive nature affects a desire for knowledge, but your knowledge of all things is supreme. Ignorance and stupidity would shield themselves with names of simplicity and harmlessness; but what simpler than you may be found, or more harmless, inasmuch as it is their own works that are the enemy of the wicked? Idleness, too, aims for a kind of repose, but what true Rest is there beside the Lord? Extravagance would be called sufficiency and plenty, but you are the fullness and unfailing source of pleasure incorruptible. **Profligacy** makes a pretence of generosity, whereas you of your great riches bestow upon us all good things. Avarice desires a multitude of possessions, but you possess all things. Envy vies for supremacy; what is supreme over you? Anger seeks revenge; what Avenger is more just than you? A **timorous** disposition shies away from circumstances unfamiliar or unforeseen or unfavourable to the things it loves, and seeks to anticipate any threat to its security. But what is unfamiliar to you, what circumstance unforeseen? *Who can separate you from what you love?* (Rom. 8.35). And where is there any lasting security, if not in you? A sullen nature is consumed with resentment,

profligacy Extravagance, especially in spending or giving.

timorous Timid, fearful, or shy.

if it loses the things on which it had set its heart; it wishes to have nothing taken from it, just as nothing can be taken from you. . . .

Book Eight

8.12.28. But when my meditation had dredged the hidden depths of my being and heaped up in the sight of my heart all the unhappiness I had known, immediately there arose a mighty squall of wind, bearing with it a mighty storm of tears. . . .

8.12.29. . . . I wept, my heart crushed with very bitterness. And behold, suddenly I heard a voice from the house next door; the sound, as it might be, of a boy or a girl, repeating in a sing-song voice a refrain unknown to me: "Pick it up and read it, pick it up and read it." Immediately my countenance was changed, and I began to ponder most intensely whether children were in the habit of singing a chant of this sort as part of a game of some kind, but I had no recollection at all of having heard it anywhere. I checked my outburst of tears and arose, taking this to be nothing other than a God-sent command that I should open the Bible and read the first chapter I found, whatever it might be. . . . I seized it, opened it, and read in silence the first heading I cast my eyes upon: *Not in riotousness and drunkenness, not in lewdness and wantonness, not in strife and rivalry; but put on the Lord Jesus Christ, and make no provision for the flesh and its lusts* (Rom. 13.13–14). I neither wished nor needed to read more. No sooner had I finished the sentence than it was as if the light of steadfast trust poured into my heart, and all the shadows of hesitation fled away.

For Reflection

1. According to Augustine, why is he writing for us, his fellow human beings? What does he want us to take away from his *Confessions*?

2. Augustine analyzes how his parents either encouraged or discouraged his sinfulness as a young person. Based on this reading, describe Augustine's father and his influence on his son. Then describe the role Augustine's mother played in his conversion.

3. The author names several vices that stand in contrast to the supreme goodness of God. In your own words, name and explain five of these vices and how they compare with God's goodness.

4. What does Augustine say prompted him to read the Bible? What biblical passage did he read, and what effect did it have on him?

23 Lost and Found

Introduction

If you ever have a chance to wander around Rome, perhaps you will find one of the great works of Baroque art in the Basilica of Our Lady of Victory: the famous Bernini sculpture titled *The Ecstasy of Saint Teresa*. This seventeenth-century masterpiece recreates in marble one of the mystical prayer experiences that Saint Teresa of Ávila (1515–1582) describes in her autobiography.

The reading in this chapter is from that autobiography, *The Book of Her Life*, Teresa's personal account of losing herself and then being found by God. In this selection she considers how easily the sinful influences around us can lead us away from a relationship with God. Teresa was born to a prayerful and devout Spanish family. She had a close relationship with her mother, with whom she shared a passion for reading romance novels. Teresa reflects on how this pastime affected her ability to act with moral integrity. Similarly, she describes how she was exposed to "conversations and vanities" in her extended family that encouraged immoral choices (chapter 2). As she recalls the negative influences in her own youth—the things she read, the people with whom she surrounded herself—she cautions us to be aware of the various kinds of vice that can shape our lives.

But as she found in her own life, regular prayer is an antidote to vice and an aid to becoming a person of virtue. According to Teresa, those who pray, even when they know they have sinned, show fortitude: "I do not know what would require greater courage among all the things there are in the world than to betray the king [God] and know that he knows it and yet never leave His presence" (chapter 8). In other words, when we pray, we display courage by confidently placing ourselves in the divine presence, despite the temptations and failures of our lives. Prayer is that strong wall of support safeguarding us and withdrawing us from the superficialities and immoralities of the world. Teresa says she is writing so that we "might understand the great good God does for a soul that willingly disposes itself for the practice of prayer" (chapter 8).

She had personal experience with this "great good." After the death of her mother, the adolescent Teresa was sent to an Augustinian convent to be educated and influenced by the nuns. Still she felt caught in cycles of sin. But when she read the *Confessions* of Saint Augustine, she was consoled by seeing God's grace at work in Augustine's life, bringing him back from a life of sin to a life in Christ. Through perseverance in prayer, she too felt reclaimed by God.

Teresa entered the Carmelite monastery in Ávila, Spain, and later initiated a reform in that religious order; those who followed her were called Discalced (or shoeless) Carmelites. Together they embraced a life of simplicity, poverty, and prayer. Prayer became Teresa's partner in all that she did, from founding convents to writing treatises on the spiritual life. Prayer was the portal into her mystical visions of God, which the Bernini statue captures in art.

As you read this selection from Saint Teresa of Ávila's autobiography, consider the important role that virtuous people play in our lives, helping us to avert the influences that can lead us to become completely lost. And take reassurance from her discussion of prayer as an effective way to find God in the midst of our faults and failures—knowing that he has never lost sight of us and awaits our willingness to be found.

Excerpts from *The Book of Her Life*

By Saint Teresa of Ávila

Chapter 2

1. . . . I sometimes reflect on the great damage parents do by not striving that their children might always see virtuous deeds of every kind. For even though my mother . . . was so virtuous, I did not, in reaching the age of reason, imitate her good qualities; in fact hardly at all. And the bad ones did me much harm. She loved **books of chivalry**. But this pastime didn't hurt her the way it did me, for she did not fail to do her duties; and we used to read them together in our free time. Perhaps she did this reading to escape thinking of the great trials she had to bear and to busy her children with something so that they would not turn to other things dangerous to them. Our reading such books was a matter that weighed so much upon my father that we had to be cautioned lest he see us. I began to get the habit of reading these books. And by that little fault, which I saw in my mother, I started to grow cold in my desires and to fail in everything else. I didn't think it was wrong to waste many hours of the day and night in such a useless practice, even though hidden from my father. I was so completely taken up with this reading that I didn't think I could be happy if I didn't have a new book.

2. I began to dress in finery and to desire to please and look pretty, taking great care of my hands and hair and about perfumes and all the empty things in which one can indulge, and which were many, for I was very vain. I had no bad intentions since I would not have wanted anyone to offend God on my account. For many years I took excessive pains about cleanliness and other things that did not seem in any way sinful. Now I see how wrong it must have been.

I had some first cousins who often came to our house, though my father was very cautious and would not allow others to do so; please God he had been inspired

> **books of chivalry** A literary form or genre that tells stories of romance, knightly adventures, and courtly love. Popular in the late Middle Ages and early Renaissance in Europe.

to do likewise with my cousins. For now I realize what a danger it is at an age when one should begin to cultivate the virtues to associate with people who do not know the vanity of the world but rather are just getting ready to throw themselves into it. They were about my age—a little older than I—and we always went about together. They liked me very much, and I engaged in conversations with them about all the things that pleased them. I listened to accounts of their affections and of childish things not the least bit edifying; and, what was worse, I exposed my soul to that which caused all its harm.

3. If I should have to give advice, I would tell parents that when their children are this age they ought to be very careful about whom their children associate with. For here lies the root of great evil since our natural **bent** is toward the worst rather than toward the best.

So it happened to me. For I had a sister much older than I whose modesty and goodness (of which she had a great deal) I did not imitate at all; and I imitated all that was harmful in a relative who spent a lot of time at our house. She was so frivolous that my mother tried very hard to keep her from coming to our home. It seems my mother foresaw the harm that would be done to me on account of her, but there were so many occasions for her to come to the house that my mother could not prevent it. This relative was the one I liked to associate with. My talks and conversations were with her, for she encouraged me in all the pastimes I desired and even immersed me in them by sharing with me her conversations and vanities. Until I began to associate with her when I was fourteen, . . . I don't think I would have abandoned God by a mortal sin or lost the fear of God, although the fear of losing my honor was stronger in me. This sense of honor gave me the strength not to completely lose my reputation. Nor do I think anything in the world could have made me change my mind in that regard. Neither do I think the love of anyone could have made me give in. Would that I had had the fortitude not to do anything against the honor of God just as my natural bent gave me fortitude not to lose

bent Inclination or preference.

circumspect Cautious or prudent.

pertinacious From the Latin *pertinax*, meaning "holding fast"; obstinate or tenacious, refusing to change.

anything of what I thought belonged to the honor of the world. And I did not see that I was losing it in many other ways.

4. I was extreme in my vain desire for my reputation, but the means necessary to preserve it I didn't take; although I was very **circumspect** so as not to lose it entirely.

. . . I was strikingly shrewd when it came to mischief. It frightens me sometimes to think of the harm a bad companion can do, and if I hadn't experienced it I wouldn't believe it. Especially during adolescence the harm done must be greater. . . . And indeed this conversation [with my relative] so changed me that hardly any virtue remained to my naturally virtuous soul. And I think she and another girl friend of the same type impressed their own traits upon me.

5. From such experience I understand the great profit that comes from good companionship. And I am certain that if at that age I had gone around with virtuous persons, I would have remained whole in virtue. For should I have had when that age someone to teach me to fear God, my soul would have gained strength not to fall. Afterward, having lost this fear of God completely, I only had the fear of losing my reputation, and such fear brought me torment in everything I did. With the thought that my deeds would not be known, I dared to do many things truly against my honor and against God.

6. These things did me harm, I think, at the beginning, and it wasn't her fault but mine. For afterward my malice was sufficient, together with having the maids around, for in them I found a helping hand for every kind of wrong. . . . I was never inclined to great evil—for I naturally abhorred indecent things—but to the pastime of pleasant conversation; yet, placed in the occasion, the danger was at hand, and my father's and brothers' reputation was in jeopardy as well. From all these occasions and dangers God delivered me in such a way that it seems clear He strove, against my will, to keep me from being completely lost. . . .

Chapter 8

1. . . . Not without cause have I dwelt at such length on this period of my life. For I certainly wish that those who read this would abhor me when they see a soul so **pertinacious** and ungrateful toward Him who bestowed on her so many favors. . . .

Venial and Mortal Sin

From the Latin meaning "forgivable," a venial sin is an offense against the will of God that diminishes one's personal character and weakens but does not rupture one's relationship with God. In contrast, a mortal sin is so contrary to the will of God that it results in complete separation from God and his grace. For a sin to be mortal, three conditions must be met: the act must involve grave matter, the person must have full knowledge of the evil of the act, and the person must give his or her full consent in committing the act.

2. I voyaged on this tempestuous sea for almost twenty years with these fallings and risings and this evil—since I fell again—and in a life so beneath perfection that I paid almost no attention to venial sins. And mortal sins, although I feared them, I did not fear them as I should have since I did not turn away from the dangers. I should say that it is one of the most painful lives, I think, that one can imagine; for neither did I enjoy God nor did I find happiness in the world. When I was experiencing the enjoyments of the world, I felt sorrow when I recalled what I owed to God. When I was with God, my attachments to the world disturbed me. This is a war so troublesome that I don't know how I was able to suffer it even a month, much less for so many years.

However, I see clearly the great mercy the Lord bestowed on me; for though I continued to associate with the world, I had the courage to practice prayer. I say courage, for I do not know what would require greater courage among all the things there are in the world than to betray the king and know that he knows it and yet never leave His presence. Though we are always in the presence of God, it seems to me the manner is different with those who practice prayer, for they are aware that He is looking at them. With others, it can happen that several days pass without their recalling that God sees them.

3. True, during these years there were many months, and I believe sometimes a year, that I kept from offending the Lord. And I put forth some effort, and at times a great deal of it, not to offend Him. Because all that I write is said with complete truthfulness, I shall **treat of** this effort now. But I remember little of these good days, and so they must have been

few; and a lot about the bad ones. Few days passed without my devoting long periods to prayer, unless I was very sick or very busy. When I was sick, I felt better when with God. I tried to get persons who talked with me to practice prayer, and I besought the Lord for them. I frequently spoke of Him.

> **treat of** Discuss or describe.

. . . For more than eighteen of the twenty-eight years since I began prayer, I suffered this battle and conflict between friendship with God and friendship with the world. During the remaining years . . . the cause of the war changed, although the war was not a small one. But since it was, in my opinion, for the service of God and with knowledge of the vanity that the world is, everything went smoothly. . . .

4. I have recounted all this at length . . . so that the mercy of God and my ingratitude might be seen; also, in order that one might understand the great good God does for a soul that willingly disposes itself for the practice of prayer, even though it is not as disposed as is necessary. I recount this also that one may understand how if the soul perseveres in prayer, in the midst of the sins, tempta-

> " *If the soul perseveres in prayer, in the midst of the sins, temptations, and failures of a thousand kinds, the Lord will draw it forth to the harbor of salvation.* "

tions, and failures of a thousand kinds that the devil places in its path, in the end, I hold as certain, the Lord will draw it forth to the harbor of salvation as—now it seems—He did for me. May it please His Majesty that I do not get lost again.

For Reflection

1. What was one of Teresa's fears that helped her avoid losing her reputation, and why? Do you find merit in that motivation? Explain your response.

2. Based on the friendships that Teresa describes in this reading, contrast the effects of good and bad companionship.

3. Teresa writes of being on a "tempestuous sea for almost twenty years." What does she say about her relationships with God and with the world during this time? How do you unite these two relationships in your life?

4. Explain what Teresa means when she writes about "the courage to practice prayer." What does it mean to "practice prayer"? From your own life or events you have witnessed, provide an example of prayer that required courage.

24 Dispelling Envy in the Soul

Introduction

An old man said to his grandson, "A fight is going on inside me."

"What do you mean, Grandpa?" asked the boy.

"It is a daily battle between two lions. One lion is evil—he is wrath, greed, sloth, false pride, lust, gluttony, and envy. The other lion is good—he is patience, charity, diligence, humility, chastity, temperance, and kindness."

The grandson thought for a few minutes and then asked, "Which lion will win?"

The old man replied, "The one I feed."

The reading in this chapter is from a sermon by Saint John Vianney (1786–1859) in which he considers our human tendency to feed the lion of envy. The evil lion in the story above represents the seven deadly sins, vices that oppose virtuous and moral living. They are "deadly" in the spiritual sense, deflecting the outpouring of God's grace and damaging our relationship with God.

In the Bible the sin of envy first appears in the story of two brothers, Cain and Abel, in the Book of Genesis (4:1–16). Cain's envy of Abel's relationship with God drives him to murder his own brother. When God asks where Abel is, Cain responds, "Am I my brother's keeper?" (Genesis 4:9). The Bible teaches that, yes, we are the keepers of our brothers and sisters—and not just our literal brothers and sisters but also our siblings in the worldwide family. As the family of God, we are created to share in one another's joy and to support one another in times of suffering. Envy destroys not only this familial bond but also the one who succumbs to it.

Born just before the French Revolution, Vianney witnessed the destruction the revolution wrought. The Church was subjected to intense criticism and was expected to submit to government control. Priests were persecuted and expelled from France. As a result, following the revolution France experienced a great shortage of priests. Vianney responded to the call to the priesthood, and in so doing he helped quench the spiritual thirst that the people of nineteenth-century France were experiencing.

Upon his ordination Vianney was sent to the village of Ars in central France. The parish of Ars had been without a priest and the Sacraments for some time. Soon he became acutely aware of destructive, sinful behaviors that were damaging the life of that community. As the pastor of Ars—Vianney is affectionately called the Curé (or priest) of Ars even today—he challenged his people to change their ways and repent of their sins. He spent long hours in the confessional reconciling people to God and one another. The transformation of his parishioners became so well known that soon people from all over journeyed to this remote village to hear Vianney's sermons and make their confessions.

In the sermon you will read here, the Curé of Ars admonishes us to put aside our pride, to examine our consciences with the help of the Holy Spirit, to reflect on how envy has insidiously entered our lives, and to seek forgiveness for overt expressions of this deadly sin. Some of the examples of envy Vianney presents reflect the conditions of his time and community, but his teaching rings true in our lives today.

A Sermon, "A Public Plague"

By Saint John Vianney, the Curé of Ars

As you know, my dear brethren, we are bound as fellow creatures to have human sympathy and feelings for one another. Yet one envious person would like, if he possibly could, to destroy everything good and profitable belonging to his neighbor. You know, too, that as Christians we must have boundless charity for our fellow men. But the envious person is far removed indeed from such virtues. He would be happy to see his fellow man ruin himself. Every mark of God's generosity towards his neighbor is like a knife thrust that pierces his heart and causes him to die in secret. Since we are all members of the same Body of which Jesus Christ is the Head, we should so strive that unity, charity, love, and zeal can be seen in one and all. To make us all happy, we should rejoice, as St. Paul tells, in the happiness of our fellow men and mourn with those who have cares or troubles. But, very far from experiencing such feelings, the envious are forever uttering scandals and **calumnies** against their neighbors. It appears to them that in this way they can do something to **assuage** and sweeten their vexation.

But, unfortunately, we have not said all that can be said about envy. This is the deadly vice which hurls kings and emperors from their thrones. Why do you think, my dear brethren, that among these kings, these emperors, these men who occupy the first places in the world of men, some are driven out of their places of privilege, some are poisoned, others are stabbed? It is simply because someone wants to rule in their place. It is not the food, nor the drink, nor the habitations that the authors of such crimes want. Not at all. They are consumed with envy.

Take another example. Here is a merchant who wants to have all the business for himself and to leave nothing at all for anyone else. If someone leaves his store to go elsewhere, he will do his best to say all the evil he can, either about the rival businessman himself or else

calumnies Slanderous statements made to injure a person's reputation.

assuage To make less severe; alleviate.

about the quality of what he sells. He will take all possible means to ruin his rival's reputation, saying that the other's goods are not of the same quality as his own or that the other man gives short weight. You will notice, too, than an envious man like this has a diabolical trick to add to all this: "It would not do," he will tell you, "for you to say this to anyone else; it might do harm and that would upset me very much. I am only telling you because I would not like to see you being cheated."

A workman may discover that someone else is now going to work in a house where previously he was always employed. This angers him greatly, and he will do everything in his power to run down this "interloper" so that he will not be employed there after all.

Look at the father of a family and see how angry he becomes if his next-door neighbor prospers more than he or if the neighbor's land produces more. Look at a mother: she would like it if people spoke well of no children except hers. If anyone praises the children of some other family to her and does not say something good of hers, she will reply, "They are not perfect," and she will become quite upset. How foolish you are, poor mother! The praise given to others will take nothing from your children.

Just look at the jealousy of a husband in respect of his wife or of a wife in respect of her husband. Notice how they inquire into everything the other does and says, how they observe everyone to whom the other speaks, every house into which the other enters. If one notices the other speaking to someone, there will be accusations of all sorts of wrongdoing, even though the whole episode may have been completely innocent.

This is surely a cursed sin which puts a barrier between brothers and sisters, too. The very moment that a father or a mother gives more to one member of the family than the others, you will see the birth of this jealous hatred against the parent or against the favored brother or sister—a hatred which may last for years, and sometimes even for a lifetime. There are children who keep a watchful eye upon their parents just to insure that they will not give any sort of gift or privilege to one member of the family. If this should occur in spite of them, there is nothing bad enough that they will not say.

. . . What a blind passion envy is, my dear brethren! Who could hope to understand it?

Unfortunately, this vice can be noted even among those in whom it should never be encountered—that is to say, among those who profess to practice their religion. They will take note of how many times such a person remains to go to Confession or of how So-and-So kneels or sits when she is saying her prayers. They will talk of these things and criticize the people concerned, for they think that such prayers or good works are done only so that they may be seen, or in other words, that they are purely an affectation. You may tire yourself out telling them that their neighbor's actions concern him alone. They are irritated and offended if the conduct of others is thought to be superior to their own.

You will see this even among the poor. If some kindly person gives a little bit extra to one of them, they will make sure to speak ill of him to their benefactor in the hope of preventing him from benefiting on any further occasion. Dear Lord, what a detestable vice this is! It attacks all that is good, spiritual as well as temporal.

We have already said that this vice indicates a mean and petty spirit. That is so true that no one will admit to feeling envy, or at least no one wants to believe that he has been attacked by it. People will employ a hundred and one devices to conceal their envy from others. If someone speaks well of another in our presence, we keep silence: we are upset and annoyed. If we must say something, we do so in the coldest and most unenthusiastic fashion. No, my dear children, there is not a particle of charity in the envious heart. St. Paul has told us that we must rejoice in the good which befalls our neighbor. Joy, my dear brethren, is what

Christian charity should inspire in us for one another. But the sentiments of the envious are vastly different.

I do not believe that there is a more ugly and dangerous sin than envy because it is hidden and is often covered by the attractive mantle of virtue or of friendship. Let us go further and compare it to a lion which we thought was muzzled, to a serpent covered by a handful of leaves which will bite us without our noticing it. Envy is a public plague which spares no one.

We are leading ourselves to Hell without realizing it.

But how are we then to cure ourselves of this vice if we do not think we are guilty of it? I am quite certain that of the thousands of envious souls honestly examining their consciences, there would not be one ready to believe himself belonging to that company. It is the least recognized of sins. Some people are so profoundly ignorant that they do not recognize a quarter of their ordinary sins. And since the sin of envy is more difficult to know, it is not surprising that so few confess it and correct it. Because they are not guilty of the big public sins committed by coarse and brutalized people, they think that the sins of envy are only little defects in charity, when, in fact, for the most part, these are serious and deadly sins which they are harboring and tending in their hearts, often without fully recognizing them.

> ❝ I do not believe that there is a more ugly and dangerous sin than envy because it is hidden. ❞

"But," you may be thinking in your own minds, "if I really recognized them, I would do my best to correct them."

If you want to be able to recognize them, my dear brethren, you must ask the Holy Ghost for His light. He alone will give you this grace. No one could, with **impunity**, point out these sins to you; you would not wish to agree nor to accept them; you would always find something which would convince you that you had made no mistake in thinking

impunity From the Latin *in* ("not") and *poena* ("punishment"); freedom from being punished or held responsible for one's actions.

and acting in the way you did. Do you know yet what will help to make you know the state of your soul and to uncover this evil sin hidden in the secret recesses of your heart? It is humility. Just as pride will hide it from you, so will humility reveal it to you.

For Reflection

1. What should we strive to do as "members of the same Body of which Jesus Christ is the Head"? What does Vianney say is Saint Paul's advice regarding this? Describe an example of following this advice.

2. In your own words, explain one of the instances of envy that Vianney examines. Then describe an occasion of envy a teen in today's world might experience, and offer advice for how to overcome it.

3. According to the Curé of Ars, how do people hide their envy from others? What are some of the consequences of this hidden sin?

4. Vianney names a virtue that helps us to acknowledge sin in our lives. What virtue does he identify? Why does that virtue help us to recognize our sins and repent of them?

25 The Cross and the Resurrection

Introduction

> SAN SALVADOR, March 31 [1980]—Street vendors were
> back on the square in front of the cathedral today and
> shoppers were strolling where more than 30 people died
> and hundreds were injured when the funeral of slain arch-
> bishop Oscar A. Romero turned into mayhem yesterday.
> . . . [A bus driver said,] "It happens this way here—a
> massacre and then nothing for awhile, and then another
> killing. We get it from every side. It goes on and on."

So begins an article that ran in the *Washington Post*. The assas-
sinated Archbishop Romero had been gunned down while saying
Mass on March 24, 1980. He died at the sacrificial altar.

Many consider Archbishop Oscar Romero to be a martyr for
the people of El Salvador, the smallest country in Central America;
its full name in Spanish means "Republic of the Savior." In the late
twentieth century, El Salvador was in the grip of an oppressive sociopolitical system, one that **marginalized** many of its people and
brutalized anyone suspected of resistance. Those who advocated
for the poor in this system did so at great personal peril. **Arbitrary**
arrests, kidnappings, mutilations, torture, rape, death squads—
the violence escalated.
Romero became the arch-
bishop of San Salvador in
the middle of this horror.
He used political resis-
tance, prayer, and preaching to fight back.

marginalized Refers to the sociopolitical
process of putting a person or group into
a position that lacks power or significance.

arbitrary Unrestrained; without cause;
based on someone's whim or preference.

The first reading in this chapter is from the Gospel that was read in Sunday Mass on March 23, 1980, the day before Romero was murdered. This reading from the Gospel of John is the well-known account in which Jesus forgives a woman caught in adultery. Her community is ready to condemn and stone her to death, but Jesus turns the tables on her accusers: "Let the one among you who is without sin be the first to throw a stone at her" (John 8:7). Everyone leaves without throwing a single stone, having looked into their hearts. Jesus, the Redeemer of us all, then calls the woman to take up a new life free from sin.

> **Social Sin**
>
> Personal sin leads to social sin. the *Catechism of the Catholic Church* explains the spiral from personal to social sin: "Thus sin makes men accomplices of one another and causes concupiscence, violence, and injustice to reign among them. Sins give rise to social situations and institutions that are contrary to the divine goodness. 'Structures of sin' are the expression and effect of personal sins. They lead their victims to do evil in their turn. In an analogous sense, they constitute a 'social sin'[1]" (1869).

At Sunday Mass the day before he died, Romero based much of his homily on this Gospel passage. The second selection in this chapter is from his homily, which has since been called "A Pastor's Last Homily." He intended this homily to confront the staggering sinfulness surrounding the people of San Salvador, but his words still call each of us today to examine our own conscience for personal sin that contributes to suffering and the loss of human dignity in our society.

In this excerpt Romero examines Jesus' forgiveness of the adulterous woman and goes on to implicate personal sin as contributing to the larger phenomenon of social sin. Salvation, he says, requires each of us to accept responsibility for our own sinful behaviors and to ask forgiveness for how we have sinned against God and our fellow human beings. But Romero also reassures us that Jesus condemns the sin but loves the sinner and will always welcome us back: "Salvation begins with the human person, with

redemption From the Latin *redemptio*, meaning "a buying back"; to redeem something is to pay the price for its freedom. In the New Testament, it refers to Christ's deliverance of all people from the forces of sin. Christ our Redeemer paid the price to free us from the slavery of sin and bring about our redemption.

human dignity, with saving every person from sin. . . . This is the call of Christ: Before all else, the human person!"

In his homily, Romero also comments on Philippians 3:8–14, also read at Mass that day. This passage from Paul's Letter to the Philippians appears as the final selection in this chapter. In it, Paul, whom Romero calls "another sinner," describes how he has left behind worldly concerns to "gain Christ and be found in him . . . since I have indeed been taken possession of by Christ [Jesus]" (Philippians 3:8–9,12). Paul tells us that it takes faith, above all, to know Christ, to recognize his suffering in our own, and to turn our lives over to him.

The readings in this chapter remind us that personal sin always has a social dimension. But when we recognize our sins and truly repent, we find **redemption** and reconciliation in Christ, who said: "Neither do I condemn you. Go, [and] from now on do not sin any more" (John 8:11).

John 8:1–11

Jesus went to the Mount of Olives. But early in the morning he arrived again in the temple area, and all the people started coming to him, and he sat down and taught them. Then the scribes and the Pharisees brought a woman who had been caught in adultery and made her stand in the middle. They said to him, "Teacher, this woman was caught in the very act of committing adultery. Now in the law, Moses commanded us to stone such women. So what do you say?" They said this to test him, so that they could have some charge to bring against him. Jesus bent down and began to write on the ground with his finger. But when they continued asking him, he straightened up and said to them, "Let the one among you who is without sin be the first to throw a stone at her." Again he bent down and wrote on the ground. And in response, they went away one by one, beginning with the elders. So he was left alone with the woman before him. Then Jesus straightened up and said to her, "Woman, where are they? Has no one condemned you?" She replied, "No one, sir." Then Jesus said, "Neither do I condemn you. Go, [and] from now on do not sin any more."

Excerpts from "A Pastor's Last Homily"
By Archbishop Oscar Romero

Personal Sin and Social Sin: John 8:1–11

The figure of the adulteress before Christ: There we have the gospel. I find no more beautiful example of Jesus saving human dignity than this sinless Jesus face to face with an adulteress, humiliated because she has been caught, and facing being stoned. And Jesus, after casting to the earth without a word the sin of her very judges, asks the woman, "Has no one condemned you?" "No one, Sir." "Well, neither do I condemn you. But do not sin again." Strength but tenderness. Human dignity before all else. . . .

The witnesses, in looking at their own conscience, found that they were witnesses of their own sin. . . . Personal sin is the root of the great social sin: This we must be very clear on, beloved brothers and sisters, because today it is very easy, as it was for the witnesses against the adulteress, to point out and beg justice for others; but how few cast a glance at their own conscience! How easy it is to denounce structural injustice, institutionalized violence, social sin!

And it is true, this sin is everywhere, but where are the roots of this social sin? In the heart of every human being. Present-day society is a sort of anonymous world in which no one is willing to admit guilt and everyone is responsible. We are all sinners, and we have all contributed. . . .

Because of this, salvation begins with the human person, with human dignity, with saving every person from sin. And in Lent this is God's call: Be converted! Individually there are among us here no two sinners alike. Each one has committed his or her own shameful deeds, and yet we want to cast our guilt on the other and hide our own sin. I must take off my mask; I, too, am one of them, and I need to beg God's pardon because I have offended God and society. This is the call of Christ: Before all else, the human person!

How beautiful the expression of that woman upon finding herself pardoned and understood: "No one, Sir. No one has condemned me."

> " *This is God's call: Be converted!* "

Then neither do I, I who could give that truly condemning word, neither do I condemn; but be careful, do not sin again. Do not sin again! Let us be careful, brothers and sisters, since God has forgiven us so many times, let us take advantage of that friendship with the Lord which we have recovered and let us live it with gratitude.

. . . In the time of Christ, people were shocked that he should speak with a Samaritan woman, because woman was considered unworthy of speaking with man. And Jesus knows that we are all equal, that there is neither Jew nor Greek, man nor woman, but that all are God's children. . . .

Jesus' attitude is what we must focus on in this gospel and what we must learn: A delicacy with reference to the person, however sinful that person may be, is what distinguishes him as the Son of God, image of the Lord. He does not condemn; rather he pardons. Nor does he tolerate sin. He is strong in rejecting the sin, but he knows how to condemn the sin and save the sinner. He does not subordinate the human person to the law. And this is very important in our own times. He has said: "The human person was not made for the Sabbath, but the Sabbath made for humanity."

. . . And so Jesus is the source of peace when he has thus given human dignity its rightful place. We feel that we count on Jesus, that we do not count on sin, that we must repent and return to Jesus with sincerity. This is the deepest joy that a human being can have.

Philippians 3:8–14

In today's New Testament reading we have another example of a sinner [Paul] who went about fooling himself for a long time, but who in coming to know Christ was saved by him and now places all his dreams, the aim of his whole life, in reaching Christ. "And everything else has become as nothing to me," the epistle says to us today. When the things of earth are no longer idolatrized, but we have come to know the true God, the true Savior, all earthly ideologies, all worldly strategies, all the idols of power, of money, of things become as nothing to us. Saint Paul uses an even stronger word, they become "like garbage," "like manure" to me, "as long as I can win Christ." . . .

Beautiful is the moment in which we understand that we are no more than an instrument of God; we live only as long as God wants us to live; we can do only as much as God makes us able to; we are only as intelligent as God would have us be. To place all these limitations in God's hands, to recognize that without God we can do nothing, is to have a sense, my beloved brothers and sisters, that a transcendent meaning of this time in El Salvador means to pray much, to be very united with God. . . .

We must continue to be mindful of how liberation must free us from sin. All evils have a common root, and it is sin. There are, in the human heart, egotisms, envies, idolatries. . . . As Christ said, "It is not what [goes into] a [person] that defiles him [or her], but rather what is in the human heart: evil thoughts." We must purify, then, this source of all slaveries. Why does slavery exist? Why is there marginalization? Why is illiteracy rampant? Why are there diseases? Why do people mourn in pain? All of these things are pointing out that sin does exist. . . .

That is why the transcendence of liberation lifts us from our sins, and the Church will always be preaching: Repent of your personal sins. And she will say as Christ did to the adulteress: I do not condemn you; you have repented, but do not sin again. How much I want to convince you, brothers and sisters, all those who see little importance in these intimate relations with God, that these things are important! It is not enough to say: I am an atheist, I don't believe in God; I do not offend him. Because it's not a question of what you believe, but objectively you have broken off relations with the source of all life. As long as you don't discover this, and you don't follow him, and you don't love him, you are a dislocated part away from the whole; and because of this you carry within yourself disorder, disunity, ingratitude, lack of faith, of community spirit. Without God, there can be no true concept of liberation. . . .

Paul says of Christ: "To know him and the strength of his resurrection and the communion with his sufferings, dying with his same death that I may arrive one day at the resurrection of the dead." Do you see how life recovers all of its meaning? And suffering then becomes a communion with Christ, the Christ that suffers, and death is a communion with the death that redeemed the world? Who can feel worthless before this treasure that one finds in Christ, that gives meaning to sickness, to pain, to oppression, to torture, to marginalization? No one is conquered, no one; . . . whoever believes in Christ knows that he is a victor and that the definitive victory will be that of truth and justice!

Church Events

. . . The Church preaches your liberation just as we studied it today in the Holy Bible. A liberation that holds, above all, respect for human dignity, the salvation of the common good of the people, and the transcendence that looks above all else to God, and from God alone derives its hope and its strength.

Let us now proclaim our faith in this truth.

Philippians 3:8–14

I even consider everything as a loss because of the supreme good of knowing Christ Jesus my Lord. For his sake I have accepted the loss of all things and I consider them so much rubbish, that I may gain Christ and be found in him, not having any righteousness of my own based on the law but that which comes through faith in Christ, the righteousness from God, depending on faith to know him and the power of his resurrection and [the] sharing of his sufferings by being conformed to his death, if somehow I may attain the resurrection from the dead. It is not that I have already taken hold of it or have already attained perfect maturity, but I continue my pursuit in hope that I may possess it, since I have indeed been taken possession of by Christ [Jesus]. Brothers, I for my part do not consider myself to have taken possession. Just one thing: forgetting what lies behind but straining forward to what lies ahead, I continue my pursuit toward the goal, the prize of God's upward calling, in Christ Jesus.

For Reflection

1. What lesson about personal sin, judgment, and forgiveness do we find in the account of Jesus and the adulterous woman from the Gospel of John? Explain your answer using details from the passage.

2. According to Romero's last homily, in what way is personal sin the root of social sin? Describe some examples in the world today.

3. Romero states an apparent contradiction: Christ "does not condemn. . . . Nor does he tolerate sin." How does Romero explain this contradiction? What does he say is most important to Christ?

4. In the reading from the Letter to the Philippians, Paul explains that he has not yet "attained perfect maturity." Based on the details in the reading, what does Paul mean by "perfect maturity"? Why does he hope to attain it?

For Further Reading

Arrupe, Pedro. *Pedro Arrupe: Essential Writings*. Maryknoll, NY: Orbis Books, 2004.

Augustine. *The Confessions*. New York: Everyman's Library, 2001.

Bernardin, Joseph Cardinal. *The Seamless Garment: Writings on the Consistent Ethic of Life*. Maryknoll, NY: Orbis Books, 2008.

Bolt, Robert. *A Man for All Seasons*. New York: Vintage Books, 1960.

Catechism of the Catholic Church. 2nd ed. Washington, DC: Libreria Editrice Vaticana—United States Conference of Catholic Bishops, 2000.

Day, Dorothy. *Dorothy Day: Selected Writings*. Maryknoll, NY: Orbis Books, 1992.

De La Salle, John Baptist. *John Baptist de La Salle: The Spirituality of Christian Education*. Mahwah, NJ: Paulist Press, 2004.

De Sales, Francis. *An Introduction to the Devout Life*. Charlotte, NC: Tan Books, 2010.

Ellsberg, Robert. *The Saints' Guide to Happiness*. New York: Doubleday, 2003.

Gula, Richard M. *The Call to Holiness*. Mahwah, NJ: Paulist Press, 2003.

———. *The Good Life: Where Morality and Spirituality Converge*. Mahwah, NJ: Paulist Press, 1999.

John Paul II. *Go in Peace: A Gift of Enduring Love*. Chicago: Loyola Press, 2001.

Julian of Norwich. *Julian of Norwich: Showings*. Mahwah, NJ: Paulist Press, 1978.

Kempis, Thomas à. *The Imitation of Christ*. Garden City, NY: Doubleday, 1955.

Liguori, Alphonsus de. *Alphonsus de Liguori: Selected Writings*. Mahwah, NJ: Paulist Press, 1999.

Mattison, William C., III. *Introducing Moral Theology: True Happiness and the Virtue*. Grand Rapids, MI: Brazos Press, 2008.

More, Thomas. *St. Thomas More: Selected Letters*. New Haven, CT, and London: Yale University Press, 1961.

Newman, John Henry. *Selected Sermons, Prayers, and Devotions*. New York: Vintage Spiritual Classics, 1999.

O'Connell, Timothy E. *The Making of Disciples: A Handbook of Christian Moral Formation.* New York: Crossroad Publishing, 1998.

Romero, Oscar. *Oscar Romero: Reflections on His Life and Writings.* Maryknoll, NY: Orbis Books, 2000.

Sheen, Fulton J. *Three to Get Married.* New York: Scepter Publishers, 2010.

Stein, Edith. *Edith Stein: Essential Writings.* Maryknoll, NY: Orbis Books, 2002.

Teresa of Ávila. *The Collected Works of St. Teresa of Ávila.* 2nd ed. Vol. 1. Washington, DC: ICS Publications, 1987.

Thérèse of Lisieux. *The Story of a Soul.* New York: Image Books, 1957, 2001.

Wadell, Paul J. *The Moral of the Story.* New York: Crossroad Publishing, 2002.

———. *The Primacy of Love: An Introduction to the Ethics of Thomas Aquinas.* Mahwah, NJ: Paulist Press, 1992.

Vianney, John. *The Sermons of the Curé of Ars.* Charlotte, NC: Tan Books, 1960, 2009.

Acknowledgments

The quotations in this book labeled *Catechism of the Catholic Church* are from the English translation of the *Catechism of the Catholic Church* for use in the United States of America, second edition. Copyright © 1994 by the United States Catholic Conference, Inc.—Libreria Editrice Vaticana (LEV). English translation of the *Catechism of the Catholic Church: Modifications from the Editio Typica* copyright © 1997 by the United States Catholic Conference, Inc.—LEV.

The quotations on page 13 and in reflection question 1 on page 19, and the excerpt on pages 13–18 are from *The Good Life: Where Morality and Spirituality Converge*, by Richard M. Gula (New York / Mahwah, NJ: Paulist Press, 1999), pages 6, 2, and 1–7, respectively. Copyright © 1999 by Richard M. Gula. Used with permission of Paulist Press.

The quotations on page 21 and in reflection question 2 on page 26, and the excerpt on pages 22–25 are from "Message of the Holy Father to the Youth of the World on the Occasion of the 15th World Youth Day," numbers 2 and 3, 3, and 2–4, respectively, at *www.vatican.va/holy_father/john_paul_ii/messages/youth/documents/hf_jp-ii_mes_29061999_xv-world-youth-day_en.html*. Copyright © LEV. Used with permission of LEV.

The quotations on pages 28 and 29 and in reflection question 1 on page 34, and the excerpts on pages 29–31, 31–32, and 32–33 are from the English translation of *Non-Biblical Readings from The Liturgy of the Hours*, copyright © 1970, 1973, 1975, International Commission on English in the Liturgy Corporation (ICEL) (New York: Catholic Book Publishing, 1976), volume II, pages 1808–1809, 96, 1808, 1808–1809, 96–97, and 974–976, respectively. Illustrations and arrangement copyright © 1975 by the Catholic Book Publishing Company, NY. Used with permission of the ICEL.

The quotations on pages 35 and 36 and the excerpt on pages 37–41 are from *Showings*, by Julian of Norwich, translated by Edmund Colledge and James Walsh (New York / Mahwah, NJ: Paulist Press, 1978), pages 125, 131, 132, 133, 149,

125, 130–135, and 139–140, respectively. Copyright © 1978 by Paulist Press. Used with permission of Paulist Press.

The excerpt on pages 43–47 and the quotation in reflection question 2 on page 47 are from *Philothea, or An Introduction to the Devout Life,* by Saint Francis de Sales (Charlotte, NC: Saint Benedict Press / TAN Books, 2010), pages 144–147. Copyright © 2010 by Saint Benedict Press / TAN Books, www.saintbenedictpress.com / www.tanbooks.com.

The excerpt on pages 54–55 is from *Francis and Clare: The Complete Works,* translation and introduction by Regis J. Armstrong and Ignatius C. Brady (New York / Mahwah, NJ: Paulist Press, 1982), pages 38–39. Copyright © 1982 by Paulist Press. Used with permission of Paulist Press.

The prayers on page 56 are from *Spiritual Exercises,* by Saint Ignatius of Loyola and reprinted here from *Finding God in All Things: A Marquette Prayer Book* (Milwaukee, WI: Marquette University Press, 2005), page 90. Copyright © 2005 Marquette University Press.

The quotations on page 61 and in reflection question 3 on page 65, and the excerpt on pages 61–65 are from *Making Disciples: A Handbook of Christian Moral Formation,* by Timothy E. O'Connell (New York: Crossroad Publishing Company, 1998), pages 10, 12, and 9–13, respectively. Copyright © 1998 by Timothy E. O'Connell. Used with permission of Crossroad Publishing Company.

The quotations in the sidebar on page 66, on page 67, and in reflection question 1 on page 72, and the poem on pages 67–68 are from *Verses on Various Occasions,* by John Henry Cardinal Newman (London: Longmans, Green, and Company, 1903).

The excerpt on pages 68–72 is from *Discourses Addressed to Mixed Congregations,* by John Henry Cardinal Newman (London: Longmans, Green, and Company, 1906).

The quotations in the sidebar on page 71 are from "Mass with the Beatification of Venerable Cardinal John Henry Newman, Homily of His Holiness Benedict XVI," at *www.pcf.va/holy_father/benedict_xvi/homilies/2010/documents/hf_ben-xvi_hom_20100919_beatif-newman_en.html.* Copyright © 2010 LEV.

The quotations on page 74 and the excerpt on pages 75–79 are from *Words to Love By . . . ,* by Mother Teresa (Notre Dame, IN: Ave Marie Press, 1983), pages 52, 54, 50–57, and 59–61, respectively. Copyright © 1983 Ave Maria Press. Used with permission.

The quotation in the sidebar on page 74 is from "Beatification of Mother Teresa of Calcutta, October 19, 2003," Biography, at *www.vatican.va/news_services/liturgy/saints/ns_lit_doc_20031019_index_madre-teresa_en.html.*

The excerpt on pages 82–85 and the quotations in reflection questions 3 and 4 on page 86 are from *The Seamless Garment: Writings on the Consistent Ethic of Life*, by Cardinal Joseph Bernardin, edited by Thomas A. Nairn (Maryknoll, NY: Orbis Books, 2008), pages 17–20, 17, and 20, respectively. Cardinal Bernardin's text copyright © 2008 by the Archdiocese of Chicago. Introduction, foreword, and arrangement copyright © 2008 by the Bernardin Center, Catholic Theological Union, Chicago. Used with permission of Orbis Press.

The quotations on pages 87 and 88 and in reflection questions 1, 2, and 3 on page 92, and the excerpt on pages 88–92 are from *Three to Get Married*, by Fulton J. Sheen (New York: Scepter Publishers, 1996), pages 1, 2, 1, 2, 2, and 1–4, respectively. Copyright © 1951 Fulton J. Sheen, Society for the Propagation of the Faith. Used with permission of the Society for the Propagation of the Faith.

The quotations on pages 93, 94, and 95, and the excerpt on pages 95–99 are from *The Autobiography of St. Thérèse of Lisieux: The Story of a Soul*, translated by John Beevers (New York: Doubleday, 2001), pages 159, 124, 113, 112–113, and 122–128, respectively. Translation copyright © 1957 by Doubleday, a division of Random House. Used with permission of Doubleday, a division of Random House.

The excerpts on pages 101–105 are from *Pedro Arrupe: Essential Writings*, selected with an introduction by Kevin F. Burke (Maryknoll, NY: Orbis Books, 2004), pages 183–187 and 8. Copyright © 2004 by Kevin Burke. Used with permission of the Institute for Jesuit Sources.

The quotations on pages 108 and 109 and in reflection questions 2 and 3 on page 114, and the excerpt on pages 109–113 are from *Introducing Moral Theology: True Happiness and the Virtues*, by William C. Mattison III (Grand Rapids, MI: Brazos Press, a division of Baker Publishing Group, 2008), pages 313, 314, 314, 315, and 312–315, respectively. Copyright © 2008 by William C. Mattison III. Used with permission of Baker Publishing Group.

The quotations on pages 115–116 and in reflection questions 1, 2, and 3 on page 120, and the excerpts on pages 117–120 are from *The Imitation of Christ*, by Thomas à Kempis, translated from the Latin into Modern English (Milwaukee, WI: Bruce Publishing Company, 1940). Copyright © 1940 by Bruce Publishing Company.

The quotations on pages 122 and 123 and in reflection question 4 on page 127, and the excerpt on pages 123–127 are from "Room for Christ," by Dorothy Day, in *The Catholic Worker*, December 1945, and found at the Dorothy Day Library on the Web, at, *www.catholicworker.org/dorothyday/Reprint2.cfm?TextID=416*.

The quotations on pages 129 and 130 and in reflection question 3 on page 134, and the excerpt on pages 130–134 are from *Scivias*, by Hildegard of Bingen, translated by Columba Hart and Jane Bishop (New York / Mahwah, NJ: Paulist Press, 1990), pages 531, 529, 532, 531, and 529–532, respectively. Copyright © 1990 by the Abbey of Regina Laudis: Benedictine Congregation Regina Laudis of the Strict Observance. Used with permission of Paulist Press.

The quotations on pages 135 and 136 and in reflection question 1 on page 140, and the excerpt on pages 137–140 are from *Edith Stein (St. Teresa Benedicta of the Cross, O.C.D.): Essential Writings*, selected by John Sullivan (Maryknoll, NY: Orbis Books, 2002), pages 74, 75, and 73–75, respectively. Copyright © 2002 by Washington Province of Discalced Carmelites. Used with permission of ICS Publications.

The quotations on page 142 and the excerpts on pages 143–146 are from *St. Thomas More: Selected Letters*, edited by Elizabeth Francis Rogers (New Haven, CT: Yale University Press, 1961), Letters 61 and 62, pages 239–244. Used with permission of Yale University Press.

The quotation on page 143 and the excerpt on pages 146–147 are from *A Man for All Seasons: A Play in Two Acts*, by Robert Bolt (New York: Vintage Books, a division of Random House, 1990), pages 141 and 139–141. Copyright © 1960, 1962 by Robert Bolt; copyright renewed 1988, 1990 by Robert Bolt. Used with permission of Random House, Inc, and Peters Fraser and Dunlop (www.petersfraserdunlop.com) on behalf of the Estate of Robert Bolt..

The quotations on page 149 and in reflection questions 1 and 4 on page 154, and the excerpt on pages 150–153 are from *Alphonsus de Liguori: Selected Writings*, edited by Frederick M. Jones, with the collaboration of Brendan McConvery et al. (New York / Mahwah, NJ: Paulist Press, 1999), pages 276, 276, 279, and 276–279, respectively. Copyright © 1999 by the Dublin Province of the Congregation of the Most Holy Reedemer. Used with permission of Paulist Press.

The quotation on page 156 is from "Vignettes of Hope," by Paul Wadell, at *www.snc.edu/communications/enews/0107/vignettes.html*.

The quotations on page 157 and in reflection questions 1 and 3 on page 162, and the excerpt on pages 157–160 are from *The Primacy of Love: An Introduction to the Ethics of Thomas Aquinas*, by Paul J. Wadell (Eugene, OR: Wipf and Stock Publishers, 2008), pages 118, 117, 117–118, 119, and 117–120, respectively. Copyright © 1992 by Paul J. Wadell. Used with permission of the author and Wipf and Stock Publishers, www.wipfandstock.com.

The third quotation on page 157 and the excerpt on page 161 are from *Summa Theologica*, by Thomas Aquinas, Question 51, Article 3.

The excerpts on pages 164–169 are from *The Confessions*, by Augustine, translated and edited by Philip Burton (New York: Alfred A. Knopf, 2001), pages 33–36, 38–39, and 181–183, respectively. Copyright © 2001 by Everyman's Library. Used with permission of Everyman's Library.

The quotations on pages 171 and 172 and in reflection questions 3 and 4 on page 178, and the excerpt on pages 173–177 are from *The Collected Works of St. Teresa of Avila*, volume one, second edition (revised), translated by Kieran Kavanaugh and Otilio Rodriguez (Washington, DC: ICS Publications, 1987), pages 58, 95, 94, 95, 56–59, and 94–96, respectively. Copyright © 1976 Washington Province of Discalced Carmelites. Used with permission of ICS Publications, 2131 Lincoln Road NE, Washington, D.C. 20002-1199, www.icspublications.org.

The excerpt on pages 181–185 and the quotation in reflection question 1 on page 185 are from *The Sermons of the Curé of Ars*, translated by Una Morrissy (Charlotte, NC: TAN Books, 1995), pages 43–47 and 43. Copyright © 1960 by Henry Regnery Company, Chicago.

The prayer in the sidebar on page 182 is from the English translation of *The Roman Missal* © 2010, ICEL. All rights reserved. Used with permission of the ICEL.

The excerpt on page 186 is from "Recriminations Leveled in El Salvador," by Christopher Dickey, in the *Washington Post*, April 1, 1980.

The quotations on page 188 and in reflection question 3 on page 193, and the excerpt on pages 189–192 are from "A Pastor's Last Homily," by Archbishop Oscar Romero, in *Sojourners Magazine*, volume 9, number 5, May 1980. Copyright © *Sojourners Magazine*. Used with permission of Sojourners, 800-714-7474, www.sojo.net.

To view copyright terms and conditions for Internet materials cited here, log on to the home pages for the referenced Web sites.

During this book's preparation, all citations, facts, figures, names, addresses, telephone numbers, Internet URLs, and other pieces of information cited within were verified for accuracy. The authors and Saint Mary's Press staff have made every attempt to reference current and valid sources, but we cannot guarantee the content of any source, and we are not responsible for any changes that may have occurred since our verification. If you find an error in, or have a question or concern about, any of the information or sources listed within, please contact Saint Mary's Press.

Endnotes Cited in Quotations from the *Catechism of the Catholic Church,* Second Edition

Chapter 19

1. *Gaudium et spes* 16.

Chapter 25

1. John Paul II, *Reconciliatio et paenitentia* 16.